The Adventures of Jimmy Olson

By

Debra Parker Oliver

David Oliver

Illustrations

Emily Oliver

Dedication

This book is dedicated by David to our daughters Jessica, Becky, and Tina. Driving nearly 200 miles each week, he told stories of the adventures of Jimmy Olson to keep their attention and pass the time. May this story remind us all of the challenges and importance of grace and forgiveness.

I dedicate the book to David B Oliver, the love of my life, my mentor, and my deceased husband. David's recovery from alcohol and his personal story of abuse is seen throughout the story. He did not get to have the reconciliation, so the story was his way of finding it. He trusted me to finish the story, and I am honored to have done it on his behalf.

Acknowledgment

This is my final promise to my husband, David B. Oliver. I promised to finish the book and publish his fictional adventure, and it took 10 years. Maintaining his story and his voice while filling in gaps was challenging.

Learning to create dreams and stories was a new experience for me. I am thankful for the readers of the story, especially our grandson Oliver Tappana, who, at age 10, was the perfect objective reader. Additionally, I thank Emily Oliver, now a graphic artist with The Oliver Rains Group, and most importantly, our granddaughter, who created the perfect vision with amazing artwork for the cover and chapters.

Debbie

Contents

Dedication i

Acknowledgment ii

About the Authors.. v

Preface.. vi

Chapter 1 1

Chapter 2 10

Chapter 3 17

Chapter 4 21

Chapter 5 29

Chapter 6 43

Chapter 7 58

Chapter 8 73

Chapter 9 91

Chapter 10 102

Chapter 11 111

Chapter 12 118

Chapter 13 121

Chapter 14 125

Chapter 15 133

Chapter 16 137

Chapter 17 143

Chapter 18 146

Chapter 19 160

Chapter 20 164

Chapter 21 176

Chapter 22 184

Chapter 23 198

Chapter 24 203

Chapter 25 208

About the Authors

Debra Parker Oliver is the Ira Kodner Professor of Research in Supportive Care at Washington University in St Louis, Missouri. The Adventures of Jimmy Olson is her first fictional story and is based upon a draft manuscript written by her late husband David Oliver. She is the author of three non- fiction books including a memoir Legacies From the Living Room: A Love Grief Equation.

David B. Oliver was a Professor of Medicine at the University of Missouri. He died while writing a draft of this story. The story represents many adventures in the life of Jimmy Olson which he told to his daughters as they were riding in the car during trips. He is also author of two non fiction books including the story of his cancer journey Exit Strategies.

Emily Oliver is a graphic designer for the Oliver Rains Group in Springfield, Missouri. She is David's granddaughter and her illustrations and the cover represent her first work with book publishing. Like her Grandfather, she is a graduate of Drury University in Springfield, Missouri with a major in graphic design.

Preface

In a story of family conflict, adventure, redemption, and forgiveness, this young adult adventure keeps us turning the pages. Johnny Westward is determined to escape his dad's drinking and abuse and his mom's complacence. He changes his name to Jimmy Olson and builds a raft, taking it down the Mississippi River to start a new life. He meets Waldo, who helps him get to Colorado. Realizing his parents are looking for him, he must escape and run to Rocky Mountain National Park. He runs into his father, Robert, in the mountains and calls Waldo for help. Waldo directs him to his brother Mike who takes Jimmy in and brokers peace with his father. Robert realizes he needs to stop drinking and, upon Mike's advice, begins to attend AA meetings.

Jimmy runs into the mountains when he thinks his Dad has again betrayed him. He falls off his horse and is critically injured. His life is saved, and his family works through healing and starting over. Jimmy once again becomes Johnny and learns to forgive his father as he graduates college, marries, and returns to Colorado to start his own veterinary practice.

Chapter 1

I stop and look around to make sure no one has seen me. I duck into the entrance of the cool cave. I stand, stretch, and smile. I've gotten away once again. I step on the soft evergreen branches serving as my carpet, walk across the cavern to my rock "chair," and sit for a moment to recover. My heart racing, I breathe deeply and begin to feel safe.

I glance over to my treasure chest next to the other wall. The locked wooden box contains my tools and the secret items I collect for my upcoming adventure. I make my way over to it and remove my watch and place it inside for safe keeping while I work. I double-checked, and my money is still stowed away.

I pick up a pile of evergreen branches and uncover a stack of logs. I have been working on making this stack for weeks. Last winter, I went on the internet during study hall and found directions on how to build a raft. Once it was warm enough to be outside, I chopped the perfect trees from all over the bluff with Dad's saw and ax. I trimmed off the branches and dragged each log into the cave for safekeeping. Chopping the ten-inch trees hasn't been easy. I've had to hide the blisters on my hands.

Finally, I found some gloves, which helped. The instructions have seven steps. I've gathered the eight long logs and two smaller logs called connectors. I've also collected rope to lash them together.

Today, I will clear a way down the bluff to the river. I walk out of the cave and glance over the bluff, trying to find the easiest place to make a path. I find a spot with no trees, just a lot of brush. I see a flat spot near the river.

Once I carry all the planks down, I can begin building. The trick will be to hide the entire scene while I build it.

I brought Dad's tree loppers so I could trim up the bushes. I clear out a foot-wide path 3 feet from the cave's entrance and begin working down the bluff. I find a stone that I'm able to dig around with my pocket knife, creating a step.

When I make it to the bottom, I stop and look around and see a flat place where I can safely build the raft. This building plot is about 15 feet from the river's edge. The river is calm here; there is no current. It should be an easy place to launch. I glance up at the bluff to see if the path is noticeable. With some strategic cover, it can be disguised. Tomorrow, I'll try bringing the first log down.

I conceal my trail and stop at the cave to put away my tools. I'll leave the loppers here tonight in case I need them tomorrow. I glance over at my stack of logs and rope. I think the hardest part is nearly done.

It's dinner time. I best leave. I better not make dad mad.

I stop at the entrance and gaze down the bluff at the Mississippi River. This cave is my favorite place; I will miss it.

I say my new name out loud, "Jimmy Olson."

I must start thinking of myself that way. I am no longer going to be Johnny Westwood. When I'm asked, I'll need the words to come out of my mouth without hesitation. I've learned the secret to telling a lie is to respond without hesitation and with confidence.

Saturday is my 14th birthday. Three days later, Tuesday, May 30th, I'm going to start a new life. No more yelling, no more hitting. I decided last year that I was going to run away after this birthday. Goodbye, Cape Girardeau, Missouri, and Mr. and Mrs. Westwood. I've got seven days to finish the raft and gather everything I need.

I'll carry the logs down tomorrow, and Friday begin lashing them together. I won't be able to do anything on my birthday because of the party. Hopefully, I'll receive the camping and hiking presents I've asked for. I'll need to finish the raft on Sunday so that on Monday, I can bring all my supplies down the hill and tie them to the raft. Tuesday is the day I've dreamed of.

Anywhere is safer than here. It's a big world and I'm going to become lost in it.

I run home; I can't be late.

My house is on the highest hill and among the oldest homes in town. My father and grandfather grew up here. It feels and smells like a museum. The porch on the front creaks as I step on it.

I stop at the door and take a breath to hide my haste. I walk into the dining room for dinner. Mom and Dad are already sitting at each end of the long dining room table. Dad glares at me and glances at his watch. I sit down on my chair between them.

Here it comes; stay cool.

"Three minutes late." I hear a sigh.

"Where did you find all that mud on your feet and clothes?"

Darn, I didn't see the mud!

Smiling, I reply, "I was playing with the neighbor's dog."

"Well, go clean yourself up and apologize to your mother for being late."

I start to rise, but I hear, "What happened to the watch we gave you for Christmas?"

Yikes! I left it in the cave!

I run to the bathroom, yelling behind me, "Sorry I'm late, Mom."

I return to the dinner table. "So where's the watch?" Dad asks me.

"I left it at Mr. Olson's house." I hold my breath.

Dad slams a fist on the table, the silverware jiggles, and the glasses shake. Glaring at me with disdain. "If you can't take care of it, then give it back to us; perhaps you're not old enough for such a nice watch.

"I love the watch, Dad. I'll take care of it. I'm sorry. It's safe with Mr. Olson. I'll be more careful."

The conversation at the table stops, and we eat in silence. Dad gulps his whiskey and pours another. The three of us sit in silence, eating. There are no words spoken; the silence is always so deafening.

"May I please be excused?"

Dad rolls his eyes; Mom stares at her plate. I rise from the table and push in my chair.

I hear the exasperated puff of air leave Dad's mouth as I turn away.

He's disgusted. I'd better get out of the way.

I walk quickly to my room.

Mom doesn't say anything. I understand she's afraid of him, but it would be nice if she defended me at least once. Is dinner like this for other families? I love dinner at Mr. Olson's. He and his wife ask me about my day; we laugh, and she even hugs me.

I hear Dad's voice through my closed door, now yelling at mom.

"What does George Olson think of such careless behavior? Johnny spends too much time over there! I don't know how I'm going to be elected between Johnny's carelessness and your inattention to your appearance?"

Mom says nothing.

Seven more days.

I walk to my room and plop down on the bed. While I feel comfortable in my room, I don't feel safe. The room is filled with books and posters of places from around the world. I stare at a poster from Colorado, where I went with Mom a couple of years ago. I dream of being there again, hidden in the mountains, Dad nowhere to be found.

I think about my plan. I've been saving money from mowing lawns as well as Christmas gifts. I've saved $1,000. I reach under the mattress and retrieve the raft-building plans I printed on the school printer. I reviewed the list I made of things I will need. I place the plans back under the mattress.

I turn off the light and fall asleep.

The next thing I know, I'm awakened by Dad yelling down the hall. I jump out of bed and tiptoe across the floor. I hold my breath cautiously, crack my door, and peek out. He's pounding on the bathroom door and shaking it. Mom's locked inside.

"OPEN UP! OPEN UP RIGHT NOW!"

I hear mom sobbing.

"Go away!"

"I'M GOING TO BREAK DOWN THIS DOOR!"

I can hardly breathe. My heart is pounding through my chest. His face is red, almost like steam is coming from his mouth.

He steps back, raises his knee to his waist, and kicks, breaking through the door. Splinters fly everywhere. This is the worst I've ever seen between them. I squint and see mom huddled on the floor in the corner behind the toilet.

Lurching toward her, I see him grab her arm and jerk her to her feet. She cries out. He takes both her arms and drags her toward their room. She's naked. I've never seen a naked woman before, let alone my mother. Her hair is wet. I assume she was in the shower. I quietly shut my door. They have no idea that I saw the whole thing.

I cautiously go back to bed and put my head under the covers. Tears creep out of my eyes as I cry myself to sleep.

The next morning, I wait to hear Dad leave for work before I go to the kitchen. I grab a cereal bar and don't say anything to mom. I fix a peanut butter sandwich, grab a bag of chips, and put them in my lunch box. I sneak the raft instructions into the lunch box. Mom is so preoccupied she isn't watching me at all. Finally, she speaks.

"I guess you're wondering what happened to the bathroom door?"

"Yeah, it's a mess."

She knows I know what happened.

"Your Dad broke through the door. I was locked inside, and I couldn't get out. He was worried about it and broke through the door to free me."

"Oh, really? I'm glad you're safe. I'm going to Mr. Olson's to pick up my watch. Sam and I are going to have a picnic at the park this afternoon, so don't worry about my lunch; I've made one."

I head out the door. I'm so tired of playing this little game where we pretend everything is OK. She pretends I don't see anything; I pretend

I believe whatever she says. We never talk about what has really happened. I can't understand why she puts up with him treating us like this.

#

Mr. Olson lives two houses down the street. He's my best friend, even though he's older than me and has gray hair. He talks to me, listens to me, and tells me stories that make me laugh. He and his wife have children and grandchildren who live in California. He likes to sit in his rocking chair on the porch, even when it is cold, reading or working on word puzzles.

Last fall, Mr. Olson and I were in his shed. I was watching him repair a leg on a table, and he showed me a large wooden spool of rope. He began telling me a story about using the rope on his farm to pull a stuck calf out of the mud. He taught me how to tie several knots, explaining the purpose of each. I knew I needed that information for my plan. I practiced making knots all winter.

Last week, I told Mr. Olson I wanted to make a rope swing and asked if I could have some rope. He gave me the entire spool and told me he had an old tire I could use. I felt guilty lying to him, but I needed the rope for the raft.

I see Mr. Olson on the porch and join him, sitting on his porch swing.

Mrs. Olson comes out of the house with a big smile. She bends down, kisses Mr. Olson's forehead, and steps over to give me a hug. She makes me feel so special.

"Here's the birthday boy! Tomorrow is the day. That was quite an

Amazon wish list, seems like you have some big summer plans," Mrs. Olson says.

"I'm hoping to receive some camping stuff for a canoe trip with my friends."

Mr. Olson appears surprised. "Johnny, that sounds fun. Who will go with you?"

Oh no, now what do I say?

"My friend Tommy's Dad is taking the two of us and Sam."

"Well, sounds like a lot of fun. I used to love to canoe."

"How's that tire swing coming along?"

"Well, Mr. Olson, I'm having some trouble, but I think I've figured it out."

"Is your dad helping you?"

"No, he works too much; it's my personal project. I'm going to ask my friends to help me hang it at the birthday party; it's our main activity."

"Is there anything I can do to help you, Johnny?"

"No thanks, Mr. Olson. I'm using those knots you taught me. It's going to be really strong."

I wave goodbye and start toward my house. When I'm out of sight, I change directions and head to the cave.

Why can't Dad be like him?

Chapter 2

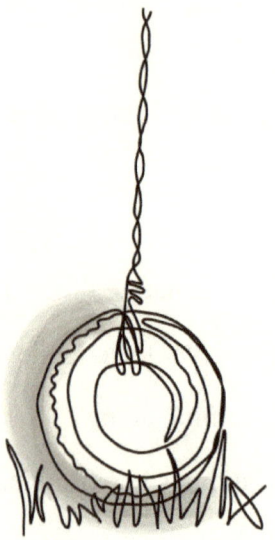

I dash into my cave and head for my treasure chest. I grab the gloves so I can work. I have a lot of work today, but I'm anxious to see my raft take shape.

I got the idea for the raft by reading a book about a guy who crossed the ocean on a raft. I figure if he can make it into the ocean, I can float down a river. His raft was named Kon Tiki. I'm naming my raft *Tiki II*.

I grab the end of the first log and pull it to the path. I look around and see no one. I start down the path, dragging it along the way. It moves smoothly behind me as I follow the cleared area, careful not to slip on the steeper parts. I set the first log down in the cleared area below, head back up for the next one, and repeat the process.

Getting the logs down the path to the river was easier than I expected; I did an awesome job making the path. I learned it's easier if I push the logs, so one at a time, I lay them out and push on one end; gravity carries them down. Only occasionally do they get stuck. Before getting the final one down, I grab my lunch box with the directions so I can eat and start building!

Once they are all down the hill, I sit on one, grab my sandwich, and review the directions while I eat. The drawing makes it look pretty easy. I'll follow one step at a time. While I'm excited, I understand it's important this raft is strong, as everything depends on it carrying me away to my new life.

I tie the outside log to one of the connector logs with a clove hitch knot.

Next, I wrap the rope around the bottom of the log two times each way, crossing in the middle and pulling as tight as I can. I make an overhand knot around the connector log. Thank goodness I printed off the pictures for reference. I repeat the process with the connector log on the bottom of the outside log. Now that I've got the frame, I can imagine what it's going to look like.

I sit on a rock and take a break. I think about my plan. I'll tell Mom and Dad that I'm going on a canoe trip and camping overnight with a friend. That'll give me a head start before they miss me. I should receive the supplies and money I need for my birthday.

I glance over at the river as it rushes by and heads off into the horizon. I watch its speed and current. It flows all the way into the Gulf of Mexico from here.

How far will it carry me and Tiki II?

I go back to work, placing the next log on the frame and wrapping the rope under the log and over the connector, like in the picture. I wrap the rope in between the logs and tighten the lashing. I do half-hitch knots between each log. After I attach each log to the top connector, I do the bottom connector.

It's getting late. I should hide my project and head back up the hill. I've gotten half the logs done today, better than I expected. I gather tree branches and arrange them to cover my work. I scatter the unattached logs around the ground so they appear like fallen trees. I'm sure no one will be down here, but I want to be safe.

After dinner, I leave the table and go quietly to my room. I take a shower and head to bed. Before falling asleep, I think of the things I still need: a life preserver from Mr. Olson's garage and a map. I'll start taking an extra bottle of water to the cave each day, so I'll have enough. I need to start sneaking things out of the house.

Tomorrow is my birthday. I'm not looking forward to the party, but I really need the presents.

#

I wake up. Today's my birthday. I've been waiting and waiting for this day. Mom put the URL for my Amazon wish list on the invitation. I asked for a small one-man tent, a backpack, a dry bag to protect my stuff on the raft, and a first aid kit.

Mom invited my three friends from the neighborhood, Mr. and Mrs. Olson, and a couple of Dad's friends. The neighborhood guys aren't close friends, but we hang out sometimes. They arrive and are excited about helping me build the tire swing. We grab the rope, and Sam climbs the tree to loop it over the branch. The grown-ups offer advice as they watch. I'm surprised that I have a lot of fun.

Finally, Bob, a neighbor who lives on the other side of Mr. Olson, helps lift the tire up high and attaches it. I'm not sure the swing looks professional enough for Dad. He probably won't let me keep it. But who cares? I won't be around anyway.

As I open gifts, I get all the things I'll need.

#

It's Sunday morning, two days till freedom. I wake up in a quiet house. In the kitchen, I find a note from Mom on the refrigerator. She and Dad have gone out for breakfast. This is perfect; I can use this time to take things to my cave. I grab a jar of peanut butter, chips, granola bars, and crackers. I find my old red wagon buried in our shed and load up the groceries, along with my new tent. I unload everything into the cave and head home. Luckily, Mom and Dad are still gone, so I leave a note saying I'm going to a friend's house for the day and I'll see them for dinner.

On the way back to the cave, I stop by Mr. Olson's house to borrow his life preserver. I noticed it in his shed when he taught me to tie the knots. He is on his front porch, reading the morning newspaper and drinking coffee.

"Hi, Mr. Olson."

"Hi, Johnny. Did you enjoy your birthday party yesterday? Your tire swing was a hit."

"We had a lot of fun. Thanks for coming, and thanks for the backpack."

"You're welcome. A backpack is important for a canoe trip. What are you up to today? You've got quite a stash of things in your wagon!"

Geez, if he only knew.

"I was wondering, can I borrow the life preserver in the shed for my canoe trip?"

"Sure, go grab it. What day do you leave?"

"We leave early Tuesday morning."

I cross the yard to the shed, yelling back, "Thanks, Mr. Olson!"

I grab the life jacket and put it in the wagon. I head toward Tommy's house until I'm out of sight and change directions. I put the supplies and life jacket in the cave and head down the path to the river to finish tying all the logs.

The final log is tied to the connectors like the first one, crossing under, pulling tight, and tying a clove hitch knot on top of the connector. I'm pumped and ready to set sail. I'll finish the preparations tomorrow and sail first thing Tuesday morning. Once again, I cover the raft with evergreen bushes and some brush. With everything hidden, I head home for dinner.

After another boring evening in my room, with an occasional loud voice outside my door, I open up my backpack and begin loading the rest of my things. I stash it under my bed. It's been a busy day. I lie down, and I fall right asleep.

#

Monday, I wake up knowing I've only got 24 hours and I'll be free.

I watch my mom, and when she goes into the living room to vacuum, I leave the house without being noticed.

At the cave, I practice putting up and taking down my tent. I need to be able to do it easily. I review my checklist and load everything into the dry bag. I head down the path, uncover the hidden raft, and tie the dry bag onto the outside log.

Tonight, I'll remind my parents that I'm going on the canoe trip. All I'll need in the morning are my backpack and my money from the cave.

I arrive home and see an open bottle of vodka on the counter. Mom and Dad are arguing, but I don't care what it's about. I don't listen. I head to my room and lay out the clothes I'll wear. Tomorrow, I'll be free. I set my alarm for 6:30 am.

It's time for dinner, and I can hear my parents laughing. I leave my room, and I find them in the kitchen. There are now two bottles of vodka on the counter, both empty.

Mom greets me with the news. "Hi, Johnny. Dad got news today. The Bar Association is going to support him running for Judge. His dream is going to come true."

"That's great, Dad. I'm happy for you."

I'm leaving just in time! I hope they drink all night. It'll be easier to leave in the morning.

15

Since they're in such a positive mood, I remind them about my trip.

"Don't forget, in the morning, I'm going on a canoe trip. We're leaving early. I'll walk over, and we'll leave from there."

"Sure, son. I hope you have a good time. Your mother and I probably won't be awake when you leave."

"No problem."

Wow, that was easy!

After dinner, I go to my room and review everything one last time. I need a good night's sleep tonight, but my heart is racing. I wonder what Mom and Dad will think, how they'll react, when they figure out I'm gone. For a moment, I'm a little sad, thinking about leaving mom.

How long will it be before they notice I'm gone?

Before going to bed, I write Mom and Mr. Olson letters. Where can I put the letter to Mom? She can't find it too soon, but she should find it once she realizes I'm missing. I consider taking both of the letters and mailing them, but I realize that the postmark will give away my location. Instead, I'll leave Mom's on my desk, sticking out of a book she knows I'm reading. She won't look at my desk until after she figures out I'm gone.

Mr. Olson's letter is harder. I decide to mail his from a mailbox on the way to the cave in the morning. It'll take a couple of days for him to receive it, even though I'm mailing it in town. Mail goes from here to St. Louis and back. I sneak into the living room, find a stamp and envelope from Mom's desk, and get back into my room without being detected.

Chapter 3

I only sleep four hours; my mind races most of the night, thinking about the trip. I'm anxious about getting out of the house successfully. I was surprised at how easy it was to remind Mom and Dad about my canoe trip last night. They never even asked which friends I was going with.

Mom and Dad are asleep as I quietly finish packing, put on my backpack, and creep to the kitchen door. I stand at the door, look back at the house, my home for 14 years, and say goodbye. I've no regrets, only relief. I close the door and head for the cliff. The sun is already above the horizon. I stop at the mailbox and drop Mr. Olson's letter in.

I walk past the Olson's home and find myself sad that I won't be seeing it again. While my home does not have many good memories, I have had a lot of fun at this place; it feels much more like a home.

I wonder what Mr. and Mrs. Olson would say if I told them the truth about Dad. They would probably believe Dad; everyone around thinks he's perfect.

I want to run, but I stop myself. I don't want to draw anyone's attention. Instead, I try to walk casually toward the beginning of my new life.

#

The sun is just above the horizon, shining like a beacon, calling me to the river. At the top of the cliff, I turn around to see the city one last time. I worry that Mr. and Mrs. Olson will be angry with me. I hope my letter helps them understand. I can't believe I'll never see them again, but I must start over.

I pick up the life preserver from the cave. I'm heading to the cave's opening when I suddenly realize I've no way to steer the raft. I'm stunned by my stupidity. I need a paddle.

After considering several options, I concluded that it would be almost impossible to steer the raft, so maybe I don't really need a paddle. All I need is a pole to keep me off the bank and away from debris on the river.

I grab my gloves and Dad's saw. Luckily, I hadn't bothered to return any of Dad's tools. I begin looking along the side of the cliff for a perfect pole. I find a fairly straight, long limb that's within reach. My spirits rise as I sculpt away the branches.

All this has cut into my time for getting down the river by at least an hour. But there's no turning back now. I finish moving the raft out of the brush and closer to the river, checking all my knots.

#

It is 8 am, and I need to get going. I put on my life vest and pull *Tiki II* to the edge of the riverbank, tying one end to the stump of a tree. The water hits me just below my knee, enough that the raft floats and I'm not too wet. I put my money into the dry bag and re-tie it securely next to my backpack.

I look out across the river. I've read the current average, five miles per hour. It looks pretty fast, much faster from here than above. However, there's only a slight ripple here, next to the bank. I'm not exactly sure how this is going to work. It looks as though the river bends left just ahead, so perhaps I can point the raft downstream and at the curve, and the river will take me to its center. My heart's pounding; I need to take deep breaths to stay ahead of my nervousness. This is it, now or never. I'm glad I can swim; I may need to swim to shore if *Tiki II* comes apart.

Stepping into the river, I lay the pole on the raft within reach and cautiously sit down on the base of the raft. My weight lowers the raft, but there's still enough water under the raft to float it. I bend over and untie the raft from the tree.

However, the raft doesn't move. I look around and realize there's a large rock just beneath the surface at the front, holding me in place. I lower the pole into the water and push against the rock. I'm moving slowly, but moving! I push off another rock. I find a slight current, and I continue to use the pole to push me out further. I begin moving faster.

I can't believe I made it! Here I come, world!

I face into the wind and river and proudly say out loud, "Oh, Tiki II, carry me far away to a new home. I'm not sure where we are going, but protect me."

#

Chapter 4

I can't believe I'm floating down the Mississippi River. Mr. Olson would be proud of me. All my planning was worth it. I'm so lucky I had Mr. Olson's help, and he did not even know it. Now it's time to use my Boy Scout river navigating skills.

Last summer, our troop did a whitewater canoe trip for a merit badge. That's where I learned a lot about how the current works, how to handle the weight of my body, how to read river navigation maps, and how to scout the shore while on the river. The Mississippi River should be easy compared with the whitewater rapids we had to deal with. There are some differences between my raft and the canoes we had, but I did a lot of research on the internet on rafting.

As I hoped, the river begins to turn, and the raft heads into the fastest part of the current. I was also right about the steering; there is no way to do it. The raft turns right and then left but, thankfully, heads pretty much in one direction, down the middle of the river. My heart jumps as I see a snake make its way across my bow toward the shore; I hadn't counted on snakes. I hate them.

Will snakes climb onto the raft?

I hear someone yelling from the bank.

"Hey there, kid, are you all right?"

It's a large man fishing from the bank. I guess I'm quite a sight; not many *Kon Tiki's* on this river, at least not in a long, long time.

What if he calls the police?

I wave and yell out, "I'm fine!"

He waves, sits down, and throws his line back into the river. I relax.

I'm finally getting comfortable with the speed; it doesn't seem so fast, after all. But it's hard to concentrate on anything else but the objects in the water. Logs, branches, a couple of plastic jugs, and I'm looking out for more snakes. There are whirlpools here and there, some big, some small. Fortunately, I haven't been swept into one, but they are scary.

I get hungry, reach into my bag for a Snickers, and swallow a bottle of water. I find my watch in the bottom of the dry bag and see that it's after 4:00 pm. Wow, I've been on the water for almost six hours.

Where am I?

#

I begin to think about how I can head over to the side of the river and stop. Until now, I haven't been afraid, except for the snake. I'm too far from shore to throw a rope at a tree near the shoreline. I look for another bend in the river; there isn't one. I begin to worry.

Is it safe to spend the night on the raft, in the dark, cruising down the river, unable to see anything?

I'm beginning to worry that I've made a mistake. Like a hot air balloon at the mercy of the wind, I'm a pile of floating logs at the mercy of the river. Suddenly, there's a huge bend. When the river turns left, *Tiki II* turns with it. Then there's another bend, this time to the right, and there, straight ahead, is a huge sandbar extending from the middle of the river to the shore. I'm headed right for it. It's as though the sandbar's urging me to come ashore. *Tiki II* hits the sand, and I grab the rope and jump onto the bar. I use the extra rope to pull the raft onto land. I'm so tired that I collapse on the sand and almost fall asleep. After catching my breath, I push the raft to the other side of the sand bar. Holding the rope, I maneuver into the shallow water and drag the raft onto the riverbank, tying it to a tree.

I find a clear spot on higher ground and pitch my tent. Peanut butter and crackers taste like a gourmet dinner; I'm so hungry. I built a small fire with driftwood surrounded by a circle of rocks, like we learned in scouts. Even though I'm tired, I need to make tomorrow's plan. I grab my map of the river before it gets too dark.

I had studied the river carefully this winter when I was preparing for the trip. There's a lot of information online about the river between Cape Girardeau, Missouri, and Cairo, Illinois. I was lucky enough to find an online journal by two guys who had floated the river a few years ago.

Examining the map, I trace the huge bends in the river, remembering the marker number I saw last, and find it on the map. I'm guessing that I'm near one of three small towns: Roth, Cache, or Klondike, on the Illinois side. I hear but don't see, an airplane flying overhead, and I find an airport on the map near Klondike. I must be near Klondike, Illinois. I put the map away, crawl into the tent, lie down on my hiker's blanket, and fall right to sleep.

"Good morning, young man," says a voice outside my tent.

I unzip the tent and glance up to see the silhouette of a large man in blue overalls looking down at me.

"Don't worry, I'm not going to hurt you. Are you all right?"

"Who are you?" I ask.

"Son, I was going to ask you the same question."

I remember to say, "I'm Jimmy Olson."

"Nice to meet you, Jimmy. My name is Bill. I work on a farm on the other side of those trees. I can't believe my tractor didn't wake you up. I'm plowing the field behind us this morning. I decided to come down to the river and enjoy putting my feet in for a bit when I saw your campsite."

I watch his eyes as he follows the rope out to *Tiki II*.

"It's my raft," I say.

"I can see it's a fine one," he replies. "Where're you headed?"

"My friends and I are in a raft race. I think I'm in the lead."

"Never heard of any raft race in these parts," he declares.

Once you've told one lie, you always have to tell another one to cover it up. Nevertheless, I say, "Oh, it's a couple of guys from scouts and me. Three of us all together. We're working on a merit badge."

"Do your parents realize what you guys are doing?"

"Sure, they're stationed at various points along the way. I saw Dad last night; he's camping upriver. Part of the experience is we have to spend one night by ourselves. I'm sure if you go back that way, you'll find my Dad. I'm doing well, don't you think?" I ask boldly.

"You sure are, Jimmy."

I can tell he's not buying my story.

"Well, I guess I'll go back to work. Good luck. I hope you win the race," he says as he turns to leave.

He's going to call the police.

Luckily, Mom and Dad are not expecting me until tonight. There won't be a missing person report for me until tomorrow night.

#

As soon as Bill is out of sight, I take down the tent and gather things together to leave. I untie *Tiki II* from the tree and push toward the riverbank. I jump aboard, use the pole to push off and begin floating again.

I need a plan, a distraction in case someone looks for me here.

Out of the corner of my eye, I spot the pieces of an old boat, broken in pieces and resting on several large protruding rocks while it waits

25

to be carried further downstream with the next rain. As *Tiki II* floats away from it, I squint my eyes for a better look.

Who owned that boat? What happened to it?

Like a lightning bolt, I have an idea. I can fake a "shipwreck." The police can find my raft, broken to pieces along the river. I can leave some clothes and food as well. With the life preserver, I can swim to shore with my backpack.

Where's the best place to do it? How do I do it? What do I pack?

The river is calm at the moment, allowing me to pull out the atlas and river map and think through where I'd like to stage the accident. It needs to be somewhere close to a town so I can go on from there. I planned to get off the river before it merged with the Ohio River at Cairo, Missouri. If I bust up the raft, I can swim to shore and disappear.

After another hour or so, I see the river marker indicating I'm nearing Cairo; I see the bridge in the distance. I take out my swimming trunks, put them on, and begin packing my backpack with a few clothes, the water, the Atlas, and, of course, the pouch with my money. I put the backpack into the dry bag to protect everything.

I set my knife aside to cut the rope holding the logs together. I put on the life preserver, strap the bag with what's left of my worldly belongings around my waist, and reluctantly begin sawing away on the ropes. I love *Tiki II*; it's the best thing I ever made. Few boys my age could do what I've done, putting this raft together. For the first time, I begin to cry.

I feel like I'm killing the raft, ripping it to shreds. I worked so hard assembling it; it took me months to finish, and some of it worked in cold weather. I loved the cave in which I planned everything, and I doubt that I'll ever see it again. As the ropes come apart and the logs begin to separate, I feel that I am leaving the past for an unknown future. It's scary.

I could stop now, save the raft, and yell to shore for help as I pass Cairo.

I keep sawing, and the logs begin to pull apart. I find myself trying to balance the remaining base, but it's disintegrating. I watch as the food and clothes that I'm leaving fall into the river. I slide into the water; it's much colder than I expected. The life preserver works perfectly, and I discover that I can float down the river much like the raft did. Then I remember the snake.

Oh no what if a snake bites me as I am getting to shore? Maybe this was not a well-thought-out idea.

I begin swimming with all my strength toward the shoreline. The bulkiness of the preserver and the dry bag tied around my waist make it difficult to go fast. I see another sandbar ahead, and if I can go further to the left of the main current, I think the bar will stop my down-river momentum. I give it a super last effort, reaching way above my head and kicking my feet as hard as I can. I shut my eyes and keep it up as long as my muscles can sustain it. Bingo! I hit pay dirt, literally. There's sand below me! I almost bruise my knees as I try to stand; the water is so shallow.

I made it.

I drop and take in as much fresh air as is humanly possible. It takes about five minutes to restore my breathing to normal. When I look up to see what happened to *Tiki II*, it's already out of sight, gone. It must be miles down the river, and although pulled apart, I hope the logs remain loosely connected. I take off the life preserver and collapse on the sandbar.

Now what?

Chapter 5

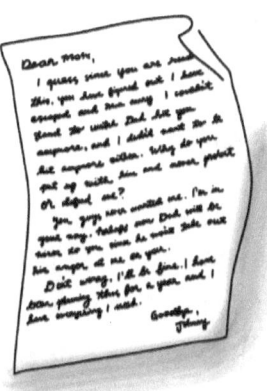

I prepare to leave the office for the day, reach for the doorknob, and pause. I take note of the plaques lining the walls, various awards for my prosecution of notorious cases, and numerous community service awards. I see my name on the door, "Robert B. Westwood, Attorney at Law," and smile. The local Bar Association has endorsed me as the candidate for Circuit Judge. Everything is off to a great start for my campaign.

Dad would be proud that I've followed in his footsteps.

I head out the door and arrive home, looking forward to a drink, dinner, and a relaxing evening. Margaret meets me at the door, concerned.

"Robert, do you remember what time Johnny is due home from his canoe trip? I can't remember if he was going to be here for dinner."

Why does she think I'll remember Johnny's schedule? She's the one staying home all day.

"I can't possibly remember his comings and goings. I'd think that's your job to keep track of him, not mine."

"Well, I'll fix enough for him, and we can go ahead and eat. He can eat when he gets home."

"He should be more responsible and tell us when he will be here. He's not considerate."

Margaret proceeds with dinner while I pour myself a drink and head to the living room to sit and relax while waiting for dinner. Margaret has dinner on the table at exactly 6 p.m. and we sit down for a nice, quiet dinner. After I finish, she proceeds to clean up, and I retire to the living room to watch the news.

Margaret comes into the living room and interrupts my show asking, "Don't you think Johnny should be home by now? I thought he would be here before dark."

I glance at the clock, and it is near 8 p.m.

"They probably pulled out of the water later than expected. I'm sure he's fine, don't worry about it. Bring me another gin and tonic."

The news ends, and Margaret again asks, "Robert, do you think we should call someone? It's now bedtime. I can't believe he isn't home."

"It's 10 o'clock, I agree he should be here. Clearly, the adult with them is not too responsible; they should have called us. Who was he going with?"

"I'm not sure, do you remember?"

Oh my God, she is so incompetent.

"YOU DON'T KNOW WHO YOUR SON WENT WITH? WHO IS RESPONSIBLE?"

"I can't remember; I didn't think I would have to. Let me think, Who could it be?"

I go to the kitchen and pour another drink. I'm not going to bed anytime soon.

"Robert, I can't remember who he said he was going with, only that he was getting home this evening. Neither of us was listening to him."

"YOU INCOMPETENT MOTHER! Do I have to do everything for this family? How are we supposed to contact our son when we don't have a name?"

"I can start calling the parents of the kids he had at the birthday party. I have that list."

How in the world is this going to look?

"What are you going to say? 'Hi, I'm Margaret Westwood, and I don't know who my son went canoeing with?' Who lets their son go on a trip for two days without knowing how to contact him? Where were they canoeing?"

"No, I don't remember that, do you?"

I'm so angry that I pour another drink and slam my hand on the counter. "I GUESS I'LL HAVE TO HANDLE THIS SO WE DON'T LOOK WORSE! Let's check the birthday party list, and perhaps we

31

can remember."

Margaret gets the list, and we begin going over the names of the neighbors. There are only four kids on the list. We narrowed it down to Tommy and Sam, agreeing that it was most likely these two boys. The question is, whose parent was going to supervise? Margaret agrees to call and asks to speak to Sam rather than his parents.

"Hi, this is Margaret Westwood, may I speak with Sam?"

She pauses as Sam replies.

"Sam, I'm surprised you are home. Sorry to call so late. Is Johnny on the way home now?"

He seems surprised. Sam must not have any idea where Johnny is.

"You did not go on the canoe trip? I thought you, Johnny, and Tommy were going on a canoe trip and returning home tonight. Maybe I was wrong, could it have been Steve or Bill that Johnny went with? Have you seen them in the last two days? Well, sorry, I bothered you. I'm clearly mistaken. Thank you, Sam."

Margaret enters the living room and sits on the chair next to me.

"Robert, something is wrong. None of the boys at the party went on a canoe trip. They are all home, and no one knows anything about Johnny."

"Perhaps it was the Boy Scouts. Did you try the leader?"

"All the boys at the party are in the Boy Scouts, and they did not say anything about a canoe trip. It wasn't a Boy Scout activity."

Now I'm getting nervous about this. It's 10:30 p.m.

Where in the world could he be?

"Margaret, go into Johnny's room and see if he wrote down the name of who they went with or any information about where they were going."

Margaret heads into Johnny's room as I think about what to do next. It would seem silly to call the police when we can't tell them who he was supposed to be with.

Maybe it was tomorrow that he was coming home, and we both got the day wrong?

I hear a scream come from Johnny's room, and I run to see what is wrong. I see Margaret on the bed, weeping, holding a piece of paper. I grab her by the shoulders.

"What's wrong? What is this?"

She stares at me, tears flowing down her face.

"Johnny is gone. He has run away!"

"HE'S DONE WHAT? IT CAN'T BE!"

I sit down beside Margaret, and she hands me the letter.

Dear Mom,

I guess since you are reading this, you have figured out that I have escaped and run away. I couldn't stand to watch Dad hit you anymore, and I didn't want to be hit anymore either. Why do you put up with him and never protect or defend me?

You guys never wanted me. I'm in your way. Perhaps now Dad will be nicer to you since he won't take out his anger at me on you.

Don't worry, I'll be fine. I have been planning this for a year, and I have everything I need.

Goodbye,

Johnny

My chest tightens. I can hardly breathe. I sit silent. I'm speechless. I carry the letter into the living room and sit in my chair. I pour another drink. I read it again. It's so full of hate and sadness, all directed toward me.

Suddenly, my memory takes over and carries me back thirty years to when I was nearly Johnny's age. I see myself sitting at the same desk that's in Johnny's room, writing my mom a similar letter, planning to run away. I see my father, face so tight, chest out, yelling at me every day. I hear my mother screaming from down the hall, as I listen through the door, the same door that Johnny must have listened through.

I pick up my drink and throw it into the fireplace.

I did this. I am worse than my father. Johnny dared to leave, but I didn't. Now, what can we do?

#

I know everyone in town. Surely, there is a quiet call I can make at 10:30 at night to see if someone can do something. He has been gone for two days, and we didn't know anything was wrong. It's now night, so realistically, no one will do anything until morning. Worse, we have no real information to provide to the authorities.

This is bad.

I have to do it. Even though it is late, we must get started. I must call the police. I'll call my friend Carl. He can keep it quiet, and I'll see if they can search and see if anyone has found a missing boy with Johnny's description.

"No, Mr. Westwood, we don't have any word about anyone missing that could be Johnny. Since he has been missing for more than 48 hours, we can put out a notice if you want to file a missing person's report. We will be on the lookout. What river did you say the kids floated down?"

"I believe it was the Current River, over near Eminence." I took a guess.

"Now, who was he with?" Carl asked.

"He has so many friends, it could be about anyone."

"I suggest you and your wife begin calling all the parents of his known friends and see if they know anything about your son and/or about a canoe trip. I think we better put out a statewide alert and include a photograph. Robert, if you can email a photo, we will send it out right away."

Should I tell him about the letter? No, he will want to see it, and I certainly can't let that out.

"Thank you, Carl, I appreciate your help with this."

I hang up the phone and pour another drink.

Margaret and I try to sleep but without any luck. I searched my mind all night, trying to remember the conversation we had and thinking of any clues. The morning comes, and I decide to head to the police station to push for some action. As I'm getting ready to leave, George Olson calls.

"Robert, I got my mail, and there is a disturbing letter in it from Johnny."

My heart races; I'm so excited Johnny has reached out to someone.

"Oh, George, thank you so much for calling; we have been up all night with worry. Would you mind coming over and bringing the letter?"

"I'll be right there."

I hear a knock on the door. George and his wife, Mary, come in and sit down with Margaret and me. George hands me the letter, and I begin to read it to myself.

Dear Mr. and Mrs. Olson:

By now you have figured out I've run away. I'm sorry that I lied to you about the rope and the canoe trip. You have been my friend and taught me many things. I'm sorry I used your rope for my raft and your life preserver. You may wonder why I've left.

My parents aren't like you. They don't talk to me like you do, asking how I am; they don't care. Dad is mean, drinks too much, and hits Mom and me. I'm sure you're surprised because he wants the world to think we are a perfect family. All he cares about is getting elected as a judge. Mom lets him be mean, and she drinks too. She never hugs me like you, Mrs. Olson.

I have prepared for a year to leave and find someone to love me. Don't worry about me. You taught me to tie strong knots for my raft. You and I had many discussions about survival in the woods, and I will remember everything you said. I got my Boy Scout whitewater rafting merit badge, and the survival skills badge so I'm ready. I'll do well by myself.

Please don't help Dad find me. If he finds me, he will kill me. How many days will it take before they notice I'm gone? I'll send you a postcard from somewhere to let you know I'm safe. Thank you for being my friend.

Goodbye,

Johnny Westwood

I am stunned. I handed the note to Margaret and put my head in my hands.

A year; he has planned this a year! He is a bright and brave kid; what have I done?

"Thank you so much for bringing this to us, George. We contacted the police last night; this is helpful in that we know he did indeed head to a body of water."

Mary comforts Margaret as she sobs in the corner.

"Robert, there are some serious allegations in his letter; what do you have to say about them?"

How do I respond to that question? I'll deflect in some way.

"George, Johnny is a sensitive kid. He is kind, curious, and has a big imagination. I'm shocked by his actions and the letter. Did you know anything about this?"

"Of course I didn't; I would never support such an adventure. There must be some reason he has chosen to do this."

"George, I'm sure you agree, the important thing is that we find him before he gets into trouble."

"Have you spoken with Joseph, Tommy's father, to see if they went on a canoe trip?"

He knows more than I do about my son.

"There was no canoe trip; we spoke with all his friends, and they were oblivious."

"Give me a call if I can help further. I'm happy to do anything. Your son is like a grandson to me. I care about him and will help in any way. Can I go to the station with you?" George says.

"That would be helpful, yes. Let's go. Mary, can you please stay with Margaret in case Johnny calls?"

We arrive at the police station. Doug, another friend, smiles and tells me he was getting ready to call me.

"There was a teenage boy found on the Illinois side of the Mississippi near Cairo last night. His name was Jimmy Olson. A farmer reported that the boy told him he was in a raft race down the river with two boy scouts. The farmer didn't believe him, and we have no information about any kind of race. Kinda strange."

"Did you say Olson?"

"Yes, that was the name."

"Did the farmer describe the boy?"

"Said he was about 5 feet, 8 inches tall, maybe 15 or 16 years old, a strong-looking kid with brown hair and blue eyes."

"That's got to be him!"

George Olson breaks in and says, "I received this in the mail today, perhaps it will help."

Oh no, I don't want that letter to get out!

I grab the letter and ask, "Did the farmer leave his name and telephone number?"

"I have it right here. His name is Bill Montgomery, and he lives on a farm near Klondike."

Doug picks up the phone and calls, but there is no answer. He said he'd try again in a half hour. George and I return home and update Mary and Margaret.

"I think that Jimmy Olson could be our Johnny."

The phone rings, and it is Doug. He spoke to the farmer.

"This sounds like Johnny. I've asked the Klondike police department to see if they can find anything, and I sent them Johnny's photo as well. They will call me if they find anything. In the meantime, someone should stay by the phone in case Johnny calls. The farmer didn't see Johnny leave and had no idea of where he might have gone. He did say the raft was gone as well. I'll also notify the police in Cairo since it's downriver. Surely, he would not have gotten further than that."

Floating on a raft in the Mississippi is so dangerous! How in the world did he make it to Cairo without crashing?

I can't just sit here doing nothing when my son is out there doing who knows what. I pick up the phone and call the Cairo police department myself.

"Hello, my name is Robert Westwood. I'm an attorney in Cape Girardeau and need some help."

Surely, if they know who I am, they will work harder to figure this out.

"I believe my son, Johnny, is the young man reported to be floating down the Mississippi on a raft and who gave his name to a farmer as Jimmy Olson. Are you familiar with the farmer's report? I understand a farmer there gave this information to your station."

"Yes, we got that report, Mr. Westwood, and quite frankly, it has made the rounds among all of us here; we have never heard of anyone in this day and age going down the river on a raft, let alone a young teenager. There is no sign of him yet, but I will add the name Johnny Westwood to the description that we have put out to all states and communities south of here. If he is on the river, we will find him for sure; I promise to call you when that happens."

I give him my cell phone number and email address. "Please let me know anything you might find out. I'm sure it's my son."

"Yes, sir, you can count on it."

Slumping back in my chair, I look across the room at Margaret. She is staring out into space.

"They will find him; he's going to be fine." She begins to cry.

Suddenly, Margaret attacks me and yells, "HE'S RUN AWAY FROM US! WE DROVE HIM OUT! IT'S ALL OUR FAULT!"

I get up and go to the kitchen to pour a drink. I pour one for her as well and take it to her. She grabs it and takes a drink. I sit down across the room in silence.

How in the world did Johnny build a raft?

Question after question comes to mind. And there are no answers. I keep coming back to "Olson." Why "Jimmy Olson?"

I should call George, perhaps Johnny has contacted him.

I call George and update him. I ask him to please stay close to his phone in case Johnny reaches out and to let us know if he hears anything. I hang up the phone and go study the atlas, and I find it missing. I'm certain Johnny took it with him; perhaps that is good. I'm sick of sitting here, so I decided to head to Cairo myself.

"Robert, where are you going?"

"To find him, where else?"

"You're not going to leave me alone, are you?" she whines.

"Yes, stay here and call me on my cell phone if there is any word from the police or anyone else. I'll call you when I've found a place to spend the night."

As I am getting into the car, the house phone rings. I quickly headed into the house. Margaret meets me at the door with tears streaming down her face. Half screaming, half crying, she says, "They found a raft, crashed on a pile of rocks, and some clothes and things!"

"Where?"

"Near a small town in Kentucky called Wickliffe, they found a life preserver. A sheriff is taking them to the police in Cairo."

"Who called?"

"The man you talked to in Cairo, at the police station."

"I'm going; you stay here, Maggie; maybe he will show up. One of us needs to be here in case he decides to come home!"

"What if he's, he's...you know, what if?" she says to the floor.

"Don't say that. He's fine. He can swim. He's going to be OK. I'm going to find him and bring him home. I'll stay in touch."

#

Chapter 6

I walk the sandbar to a bank of grass ten or so yards away. I realize I forgot to undo the dry bag and check on my backpack inside. I checked to see if everything stayed dry. The bag is supposed to be waterproof.

Dry as a bone!

I stretch out on the ground. Once my swimming suit is dry from the sun I will change into my shorts and polo. I close my eyes for a second and fall asleep. When I awake, my skin feels warm. I see red skin. My face and the front of my body, nearly head to toe, are burning.

I forgot the sunscreen. I take off my swim trunks. I put them in the water and apply the cool trunks to my face. The cool water helps a bit. I put on dry shorts and a shirt and begin to think about what is next.

Interstate 57 runs into Cairo. I can hitchhike from there. The sun will go down soon. So I need to get busy finding the highway.

I can feel my skin stretch tight across my body and face as I climb up the embankment. I venture across the big grassy field, watching for snakes along the way. I enter a field of corn that is about a foot high. Mom and I used to take drives into the country around Cape. I think she liked to go on those drives to stay out of the house, to escape from Dad.

Dad knows by now. He must be so mad. I hope he doesn't take it out on mom.

I see a row of trees and some power lines at the edge of the field. It is a long way away, but I think it is a road.

Should I keep using Jimmy Olson as my name?

I don't think that farmer bought my story. I worry he will tell the authorities.

Dad will figure out Olson.

He knows I spend a lot of time at Mr. Olson's house. I like the name, and it's easy for me to remember and respond to naturally. I decide to keep using it. I must be nearly fifty miles from home by now. When I get to that road, I'm going to keep going south. I'm sure the South is to the right and I want to go further and further away from Cape.

I reach the road, and daylight is vanishing fast. I turn right, and once on the asphalt, I pick up my pace. The road seems to follow the path of the river, so I should reach I-57 soon. In case I'm wrong, I begin to look for safe spots to spend the night. I don't have to worry about getting cold; with this sunburn, it will feel good. My legs are getting tired, and my back is sore from swimming to shore.

"There it is!"

It's much closer than I thought it would be. My spirits rise. I hear a vehicle coming around the bend behind me. I jump into the ditch beside the road and hunker down. I pray he doesn't stop. I can't afford to be seen now; too many questions to answer, too many lies to tell. He drives right on by. I climb quickly out of the ditch. I walk as fast as my sore body will go toward the bridge. Surely, I'm the only homeless person in these parts. I'll be upset if someone else has claimed a home under the bridge. I crawl up the concrete incline to a level space. When a truck passes, I hear the tires whining in the distance before it gets here.

As it approaches, the noise grows deafening, and the bridge shakes. I begin to doubt if this is the best place, but I'm too exhausted to worry. My body is burning from the sun. I stretch out and use my backpack as a pillow.

A loud truck wakes me. My skin is tight across my face and tender to the touch. I feel like I'm on fire. My legs aren't so bad. I'd love to have some lotion, but I'll have to grin and bear it. My whole body is sore. I'm so thirsty I'm afraid I'll drink the last of my water. I have two bottles and part of a third. I down the partially filled bottle. I have one can of soup left. I open it with my knife and drink it down cold. Another peanut butter sandwich seems to do the trick for breakfast. I relieve myself in the bushes to the side of the embankment, sit down, and open my Atlas.

Which way should I go? What will they expect me to do?

To the North, I-57 eventually reaches Chicago; to the south, after connecting with I-55, the end of the line is New Orleans.

So which is it? The Great Lakes or the Gulf of Mexico?

I ponder this for a while. With each passing truck, I feel like I'm missing rides. If they find the raft and connect it with a potential report from Fred, the farmer and find a piece of clothing or two, they'll probably assume I'll continue south. So I think I should go north. I'll try to hitch a ride toward Chicago.

I need a Wal-Mart to buy some lotion for my skin, deodorant, food, and more water. I am also craving some fruit, maybe an orange, apple, banana, or all three. Thinking of food, I climb up on the highway, find the sun in the east, and decide that I'm on the right side of the road to go north. I put my thumb up like I saw on TV and smile. I'll need a believable story, so I'd better think fast. The next truck starts slowing down.

#

I move off the shoulder of the highway while the truck pulls over. I can see the driver is a large man. The truck is huge. It doesn't have any markings. He reaches over, opens the passenger door, and motions for me to climb up. I have to pull on some handles to hop into the cab.

"Well, son, where you going?"

"Champaign, Illinois."

"Well, it depends on how far you're going. I look forward to hearing what brings a young man out here in the middle of nowhere."

He doesn't believe me. He knows I'm running away!

I should jump out of the cab right now.

"I'm going to be a freshman at the University of Illinois. I'm enrolled in summer school classes. I don't have much money, so I decided to try hitching a ride. Are you going that far?"

He seems to relax.

I think it worked!

I'm so glad that I studied the atlas. Just this morning I saw the University of Illinois in the Champaign Urbana area. The college thing came out of nowhere.

"I'm going to Danville, Illinois. I'll be leaving this Interstate 74, so you're in luck because I catch it at Champaign-Urbana. What do you plan to study at the University?"

"Agriculture."

"You look awfully young to be going to college."

"Everyone says that I've got a baby face."

"Well, how long have you been standing by the highway? You look roasted!"

"A long time. I live in Cairo; several of my friends told me that walking down to the Interstate and catching a ride is easy. This is the first time I've tried it. Yesterday, I stood there all day, but no one stopped, so I thought I'd try it one more day. I'm glad you came along first thing."

"Well, I figured you for a runaway. I ran away from home when I was young but gave it up after two days. I've often wondered what would have happened. Why agriculture?"

"My Mom grew up on a farm, and she taught me about crops. It fascinates me."

"What about your dad? What does he do?"

"He's gone. One day, he up and left us. I was six years old, and although she doesn't believe me, I remember the day he left. He was drunk, Mom was afraid, and I was hiding at the top of the stairs listening. I saw everything. Mom and I were afraid of him. He always got violent when he had too much to drink."

I'm on a roll now, and all this is easy to tell since most of it is true.

"He hit my mother across the face, and she yelled at him. He left that day. What I can't understand is why Mom misses him."

"Have you seen him since then?"

"No, and that's fine with me. I got a scholarship to Illinois."

"You don't say!"

"Yeah, I'm nervous about going to a big university."

"There's a truck stop ahead, and I plan to buy gas and something to eat. By the way, my name is Waldo Emerson. What's your name?"

"Jimmy Olson. Were you named after the famous poet Ralph Waldo Emerson?"

"Nope, never heard of him."

Several miles up the highway, we pull into the truck stop, and after parking, we both head for the restroom.

He pumps gas while I look around the huge store. I find some lotion and three candy bars. I go back in the restroom, pull up my shirt, and splash cold water all over. I then apply the lotion to my body. Wow, it feels good. Feeling refreshed, I went to the restaurant where Waldo told me to meet him. I order a large soda and wait.

Waldo approaches the table. He's bigger than I thought.

"So what sounds good, Jimmy?"

"I'm hungry. I want the largest hamburger they make and a vanilla milkshake."

"I'm a steak and potatoes man; I'm going to have me a Ribeye."

I look at him, not knowing what to say next. There's a bit of uncomfortable silence, and he leans over and almost whispers, "So, Jimmy, where are you really going?"

I stare at him.

How much do I trust him? He said he ran away once.

He waits. I'm amazed by his patience. I feel like running, but that'll get me nowhere. I realize that I've got to tell him the truth and take my chances. Our food arrives, and as we eat, I tell him everything.

The drunken stupors, the violence, and the physical and emotional abuse were all going on in our home. I explained that no one, absolutely no one, on the outside has a clue to his behavior and treatment of my mother and me. I leave out nothing. The busting through the bathroom door with splinters flying everywhere and the spankings that I often got with a belt. I even told him about the yelling and screaming that made me run to my cave.

I proudly told him about building the raft. I tell him how I made it appear that *Tiki II* came apart and I drowned.

"Please don't turn me in, Waldo. My Dad will kill me."

A long silence separates the two of us. I wait. I see that he is thinking about what to say or do. My immediate future hangs in the balance. If I were in his situation, I'd have no idea what I would do. He leans forward to speak. I'm tense, holding my breath, my stomach is tight.

"OK, Jimmy, I have a deal I want to make with you. I'm doing this only because I regret not sticking to my plans when I had the chance to run away from my home. I should've kept on the run. I think I would be doing something other than driving a truck if I had stayed the course. You have been brave. I can't believe how much planning you did and how much you prepared to leave home; it is remarkable. Stay here, I'll be right back, I need to grab some paper and a pencil."

I am speechless. He gets up and heads for a server standing at the cash register. I can see him negotiating for the paper and pencil and buying a postcard.

A deal? I have no idea what kind of deal he might offer me.

He returns to the table with a serious look on his face. He sits down, centers the paper in front of him, writes something, and hands me a postcard.

"Here's the deal. If you're going to the University of Illinois, I'll drop you off there, and we'll never see or hear from each other again. But I think you made that up; you are not old enough to go to college, and you have no idea where you are going. Am I right?"

Do I go ahead and tell him I've no idea where to go now?

For some reason, maybe because Waldo has been so nice to me, for once in my life, I don't want to lie. I look him squarely in the eyes.

"I'm not sure where I am going, perhaps Chicago, but everything else I told you about my family and building the raft is true."

"OK, I thought so. I'm proud of you, Jimmy, for telling me the truth, and I'm counting on you to be honest with me when you hear my proposal."

"Let's hear it."

"I'll take you to a bus station; you can buy a ticket to wherever you want to go but you must promise me two things."

"What is it?"

"First, you must write something on this postcard so we can send it to your mother. She must be worried sick, and she needs to know you are ok. I'll mail it far from here so she will think you are going in the opposite direction from where you are. Secondly, I'm going to write my name on this piece of paper, the address of my home, my phone number, and also my email address. You must promise me that if you have any trouble and want to call it off, you'll contact me. Can I trust you to do that?"

Is he kidding? That's it? No sweat.

We seem to have some kind of common bond.

"Waldo, I've told a lot of lies in my life, but I'm not lying to you. I promise to contact you if I need help."

He is looking at me right in the eyes. He nods his head in agreement.

"How can I ever thank you, Waldo?"

"Being true to your word is all you have to do. I don't care if you call or contact me tomorrow or in a week, a month, a year."

"OK, I promise."

"Take this pen now and write something to your mother."

I take the pen, think for a couple of minutes, and write.

Dear Mom,

I want you to know I'm safe and doing ok. I'm making friends and finding people who are nice. Don't let Dad blame you for my leaving. It's all his fault.

Love,

Me

I don't want Waldo to know my name is not Jimmy.

I put Mr and Mrs Olson's name and address on the postcard and I handed the card to Waldo. He puts it in his pocket.

"Jimmy, every now and then, I'd love to hear from you, hear what you're doing, how you are doing. It's not part of the deal, but if you'd do that, it would really please me."

"I'll put your information in a safe place. Guard it wherever I go,

Waldo. I promise to stay in touch. Thank you so much!"

"So, where do you want to go?"

I didn't think I'd make it this far and now I have the opportunity to go further away.

"I want to go to Colorado."

"That's a big state, where to?"

"Maybe a bus to Denver, and then I can catch a shuttle up to one of the resorts."

I remember getting from place to place in the mountains on shuttles they went everywhere.

"All right, here's the plan. I'll take you to the Greyhound Bus Terminal in St. Louis, and we'll buy you a ticket to Denver."

"Yes, that makes sense."

"There is a catch. Since you are fourteen years old, a soon-to-be freshman in high school, and you don't have a driver's license or any other identification, I'll go in the terminal with you and say that you're my son and that I want to buy a ticket for you to Denver. Do you have any money?"

"Yes."

"I'm going to give you $100 to help. That should allow you to catch the shuttle and to stay at a hostel for young people for a week or so and for food. Do you know what a hostel is and how to find one?"

"A hundred dollars?"

"Jimmy, you'll need to learn that it is expensive living on your own. I hope you find a job right away, and promise me you'll let me know. When you arrive, I want to know your whereabouts, your situation, and how much money you have left, OK? Again, do you know what a hostel is?"

"Don't worry about me, Jimmy. I drive this truck all across the country for a living. Shucks, I live in this thing. A short spin over to St. Louis is nothing, and who knows, I might end up with a contract to deliver some goods to Colorado, and we could meet up again."

"Thanks, Waldo; I appreciate everything."

After returning to the truck, we drive for quite a long time, saying nothing. I'm thinking about my bus ride to Denver. I bet he is reliving running away from his home or wondering if he should really be doing this. I wonder if he is going to change his mind. What if the police are looking for me? I wonder if Dad really cares and if Mom is doing OK. There are so many things to think about. I can't believe I've made it this far.

"Jimmy, if I end up in trouble for helping you, all I ask is that you say that you asked me to drop you off at the bus station in St. Louis. Would you be OK saying that?"

"Of course, and it's the truth."

"Thanks, I believe I can count on you."

We roll into St. Louis around 2 p.m. and find a bus that goes to Denver for $144.00. Waldo pays for all of it! He won't take any money from me and tells me to forget it. Well, I'll never forget it. And he was right about a long ride, eighteen hours. He tells me to try to sleep during the night and that I'll need lots of energy to find and negotiate a ride to one of the resorts.

We walk into a café across the street and sit in a booth by the window. We order cheeseburgers.

"Jimmy, you need to be careful and remember that not everyone you meet will be nice; there are some evil people who would do you harm."

"I don't bother anyone, so I don't think they will bother me."

"The world doesn't work that way. Some people are out to take advantage of you or will steal from you, so don't trust everyone."

"I'll be on guard, Waldo. I guess trust must be earned. You don't have to stay here and wait with me. I can catch the bus. I'm sure you have to get to where you are going."

"I'll feel better if I see you off. I'm sure after everything you have managed to do, getting on the bus is easy, but humor me and let me make sure you are headed in the right direction."

"Waldo, do you have any family?"

"I have a son, but I haven't seen him in a few years. His mother took him and left and I have never found them. He would be about your age. I hope he's as good a kid as you, Jimmy."

"That is so sad; why would she do that?"

"It's a long story. Maybe I wasn't as good a husband and father as I needed to be. Perhaps she found someone else. She didn't leave me a note and never called. I left for a trip across the country, and she quit answering the phone. When I got home, everything in the house was gone, and so were they. Tore me up inside. I wish I could have seen my boy grow; he was only 6 years old at the time."

"Wow, so sad. Do you have any other family?"

"A brother in Estes Park, Colorado. We were close as kids. We had to take care of one another because our dad was so mean. My brother started drinking as soon as he left home, and we drifted apart. I only talk to him once in a while now. We better get you on that bus now so you can pick a good seat."

We walk over to the bus, and Waldo gives me a huge bear hug. I see a tear in his eye.

"Godspeed, Jimmy. I wish you the best; remember to stay in touch. I'll be thinking about you and worried, so please let me know if you are OK. I'm a phone call away if you need anything."

"I will."

I walk up the steps of the bus. I feel like crying, too, but I've got to concentrate on where to sit. I'm hoping the person next to me is someone I like. I have to remember to be careful in trusting people.

I take a window seat and see Waldo walking away. I hope I see him again; I'll keep in touch. I'm thinking about all the things he told me about people on buses, downtown Denver, finding a shuttle and a hostel, and more.

My skin is still burning from the sunburn; I should have gotten some lotion before getting on the bus. I try to think about something else and get lost in thought when a nice-looking old man sits next to me. He takes up little room puts his few things above the seat next to where I'd already placed my bag.

As he sits down, he introduces himself. "Hi, young man. My name is Sampson, James Sampson. You can call me James."

"Hi. My name is Jimmy Olson; you can call me Jimmy."

"Two Jims; that will be easy to remember, Jim and Jimmy. How far you going?"

"Denver."

"Me too."

"I promise not to snore too much if you do the same."

He has a nice smile. I am lucky to have such a perfect seat companion for the long ride.

"I'm not sure if I snore or not, but if I do, pat me on the back, and I will shut up." He takes out a sandwich and starts eating it. I do the same with a chicken wrap that Waldo bought me for the trip; he said it was my going away present.

Chapter 7

Margaret is waiting on the porch for me as I pull into the driveway. I explained that Johnny was most likely on a raft heading down the Mississippi River and somewhere north of Cairo. I explained that he had talked to the farmer who had seen a boy who was surely Johnny. She nervously listens as I describe what little information I have.

I need to call the police station in Cairo, Illinois. As the phone rings, I tell her, "Johnny told the farmer his name was Jimmy Olson, but it was obviously our Johnny!" Margaret stares straight ahead.

"Hello, my name is Robert Westwood. I'm an attorney in Cape Girardeau and need some help."

"I believe my son, Johnny, is the young man reported to be floating down the Mississippi on a raft and who gave his name to a farmer as Jimmy Olson. Are you familiar with the farmer's report?"

"Yes, we got that report, Mr. Westwood. Quite frankly, it has made the rounds among all of us here. We have never heard of anyone these days going down the river on a raft, let alone a young teenager. We haven't seen any sign of him yet. I'll add the name Johnny Westwood to the description. We've sent the information to all states and communities south of here. If he is on the river, we will find him. I promise to call you when that happens."

"Please call me about anything you might find out. I'm sure this Jimmy is my son."

"Yes, sir, you can count on it."

Sitting in my chair, I look across the room at Margaret. She is still staring out into space.

"They will find him. He's going to be fine."

"He's run away from us! We drove him out! It's all our fault."

I try to remain calm and sit back in my chair. Someone has to stay in control, and clearly, she is not.

Could it be my fault? What if we don't find him?

I tell myself it's impossible that a kid can do this and not be found.

"Go get me a drink so I can think!"

How in the world did Johnny build a raft? Who helped him? How long has he been planning this? What did he take with him? Does he have any money?

Why Jimmy Olson?

I reach George Olson's house and ring the doorbell. George opens the door, "Hello, Robert, come on in. What can I do for you?"

"What did you do to help him? How could you support a fourteen-year-old kid in his effort to run away? We know he visits here often. Do you have any idea what he is up to? Did you help him build some kind of raft?"

"Robert, I know you're upset, and I'm concerned as well. Let's talk about this man-to-man. Come in and tell me more. I'll do anything I can to help you."

I sit down on the sofa and begin to bring him up to date.

"Robert, hindsight is, of course, 20-20. Johnny is a bright and curious young man who asks a lot of questions. Clearly, he was asking because he was working on a plan. I assure you I didn't have a clue. If I had known what he put in that letter, I'd have handled those questions differently."

Is he threatening me?

"Johnny never seemed any different than any other fourteen-year-old kid. He wanted to learn to tie knots, so I taught him. He wanted to make the rope swing, so I gave him what he needed. He told me he was going on a canoe ride with friends, so I gave him the life preserver. I thought nothing about it."

He seems sincere.

"Clearly, Johnny was listening to everything and has used all that in this plan. I guess you had no reason to think anything of it. I apologize. As you can imagine, I'm terribly worried."

"If there is anything that Mrs. Olson or I can do, please let us know.

We love Johnny and are willing to help in any way."

"Thank you. We will keep you informed."

I walked back home and into the house. There was a bottle of vodka on the counter, and Margaret was having a drink. I go and pour myself one as well. I deserve it. I remember I have another map in the study drawer; perhaps it will give me some ideas.

I notice that all the towns south of Cairo are small. Memphis is the next large city. I check the roads that follow the river; Johnny is heading south.

I pack a bag. I can't wait for the phone to ring. I call my law partner to tell him I'll be gone for a couple of days. I don't tell him why. Surely, I can get this wrapped up without a lot of publicity.

"Where are you going?"

"To find him, where else?"

"You're not going to leave me alone, are you?"

"Yes. You stay here and call me on my cell phone if there is any word from the police or from anyone else. I'll call you when I have a place to spend the night."

The house phone rings just as I shut the door. I hear it and pause. After a couple of minutes, I step back inside to check on the call. Margaret meets me at the door with tears streaming down her face. "They found the raft crashed on a pile of rocks!"

"Where?"

"Near a small town in Kentucky called Wickliffe, and they found a life preserver and some clothes. A sheriff is taking them to the police in Cairo."

"Who called?"

"The man you talked to in Cairo, at the police station."

"I'm going. You stay here, Maggie; maybe he'll call."

"What if he's, he's…, what if?"

"Don't say that. He's fine. He can swim. He's going to be OK. I'm going to find him and bring him home. I'll stay in touch."

#

I glance down at my speedometer, and it reads 90 mph. I glance around and check my mirror for any highway patrol officers and decide to keep pushing it.

The drive gives me time to think. Suddenly I have a flashback moment of a night when I was about Johnnys' age. I am in my room after dinner and hear a scream in the living room. I open my door and sneak quietly down the hall until I can see the living room. I hear my parents arguing. I remember seeing the rage in my father's eyes as he grabbed my mother's arm and pulled her from the chair. She was crying. I was so scared I turned around and went back into my room. I buried my head under the pillows. I'd forgotten all about that night.

I bet Johnny was afraid of me like I was my father.

I pull into the parking lot, park, and rush into the small police station. I'm introduced to the officer on the case. He turns around and lifts a life preserver and a tee shirt.

"Do you recognize these?"

"Oh my God, he borrowed this life preserver from our neighbor, and this tee shirt is Johnny's. Do we know if he is ok?"

"Mr. Westwood."

The officer then motions for me to follow him down the hall and into another room. It is full of all kinds of assorted things. "This is where we keep evidence and other items that we pick up on the various cases that we investigate."

He pulls forward a log and rope tied to it. "Do you notice anything unusual here?"

Bending over and picking the log off the floor, I look at the rope tied to it. Looking closely, I notice what he's referencing.

"It looks cut."

"That it docs, and if you pull around the other end, you will see that it is cut too, most likely by a knife. We think your son staged the destruction of the raft. It appears that he cut the rope and hoped that it would appear like he drowned. Is your son running away, Mr. Westwood?"

The next 15 seconds seem like an hour as I scramble for an answer. I am suddenly overwhelmed with emotion. My heart races, my chest gets tight, and I fight back tears in my eyes. I can't let him know the truth.

"I don't know what the boy was thinking, officer. I raised him to be better than this. I'm disappointed in him. I'm sorry for all the trouble he is causing."

"Did you and your son argue? Did he get into any trouble recently? Did he seem angry at you or your wife?"

"No, sir, we are an average family. We had a big birthday party for him, and everything seemed fine. Do you think someone might have taken him?"

"Mr. Westwood, we have no reason to believe there is anyone else involved in this unless there is something you aren't telling us."

"The reason isn't important; we need to focus on finding your Johnny."

I take a deep breath and agree there is no time to be lost. The police officer gets out a map and points.

"If he climbed out of the river near the break-up of the raft, his options would be fairly limited. Although we are not sure how far the raft traveled before coming apart. We'll check the bus stations. We'll send the missing persons bulletin out statewide as well as in the bordering states. I was about to drive up and show that picture of Johnny to the farmer north of here. Hopefully, he can get an identification."

I ask if I can go with him and he agrees. We pull up in front of the farmer's house. The front door opens and the farmer greets us on the front steps.

"Glad you made it, officer; let's see that picture."

The officer hands him the picture.

"That's him, all right. Strong, but I never believed his story about some sort of raft race down the Mississippi. What happened to him?"

"We found the raft on some rocks, but no boy.'"

"You gonna search the river for a body?"

"No, not yet; we think he made it to shore."

"I'm sorry. Are you the kid's father?"

"Yes."

"Well, Mr. Olson, sorry this is happening."

I tighten my fists.

"I'm not Mr. Olson. I am Mr. Westwood, and my son's name is Johnny."

"Why would a kid that young be running away and changing his name? Did you do something to him, Mr. Westwood? He may be seriously hurt. How could you let this happen? Did you not notice he was missing? Seems to be the kid had reasons of some kind for risking his life."

I exit the car, walk over and stare at him.

"How dare you accuse me of anything. How could you have walked off and let him walk away if you thought something was wrong? I think this is your fault."

"Don't blame me for your trouble. You should be thanking me."

Next thing, the officer stepped between us. I wanted to blame the guy for being so rude and letting my boy go!

"Mr. Westwood, we understand you are worried. Let's go back to the car and find your son."

I relax and sit back in the car. The farmer turns and goes back into his house.

#

I drive home, trying to understand the events of the last 24 hours.

Was I so awful he had to run away? I've got a temper, but I didn't think it was as bad as my father's. He made all these plans and now wanted us to think he was dead.

I pick up the phone and call Margaret and give her the details. I fight back tears.

Margaret is waiting at the door when I arrive home.

"I need a drink. I'm exhausted. This is all insane. I can't believe he has been so stupid and reckless. This looks so bad for me. He has no respect. Make that a double."

I drink it down and Margaret grabs me another. She spills it as she hands the second drink to me.

"How can you be so careless? This is your fault. If you were a better mother, he wouldn't have run off. I can't believe you didn't know who he was going with. How many times did you let him go off somewhere to build that raft? Any decent mother would have known what their son was doing."

She turned around quickly and slapped me! She let out a scream.

"DID YOU NOT READ HIS NOTE? THIS IS YOUR FAULT, NOT MINE!"

"How dare you accuse me of this?" I slapped her as hard as I could

66

for saying such a terrible thing.

Margaret fell to the floor, sobbing. I drink my second drink and head to the kitchen to make another. I return, and she's still on the floor.

"You think that crying is going to make anything better? Get up and at least start my dinner."

I sit in my chair and I turn on the news. I recall the conversation at the police station. What if Johnny is hurt? Where is he? What if something happens to him? What if he never comes home? How am I going to explain this to everyone?

I walk into his room and look around. This room was once my room. I sit on the bed and remember hearing my parents fight and hiding under the covers. I can see Johnny doing the same thing. I recall the fear I had of my father's rampages. I must have scared him the same way. I throw my drink against the wall in frustration. Margaret walks in.

"What are you doing? Why did you throw that drink?"

"I'm not hungry. I'm going to bed."

"Don't you even care your son is out there somewhere? How can you ignore this and drink it away? I'm going over to the Olsons'."

"I don't care what you do; stay away from me."

I go to bed. I can't hold the tears back any longer. I sob into my pillow. I'm glad Margaret is gone. I fall asleep.

#

I wake up a couple of hours later and walk into the living room.

Margaret is sitting on the couch. Her eyes are red.

"I'm sorry, I should not blame you. It's all my fault. If something happens to him, I will never forgive myself. From now on, I'm going to be a better father and a better husband. When we find Johnny, I promise to be a different person. You won't recognize me, Maggie."

I sit beside her and we hug and break down in each other's arms. I realize an apology is not sufficient this time. There are no words to fix this one.

"Robert, I forgive you for blaming me, but if something happens to Johnny, I don't think I can ever forgive you. I'm also at fault because I've put up with your drinking and abuse for too long; I didn't protect him. No child should have to have witnessed and experienced what he has."

"I realize that because, sadly, I went through the same thing. I realized, sitting in his room, that I was in that same room as a child, feeling the same way. How could I have done this to both of you? I'll never touch another drink again. I promise."

"If you do, I promise I'm leaving you. I'll never let you hurt either Johnny or me again. I love you, but I can't live with how you treat either of us. I'm done with it. We need to focus on getting Johnny back."

"It's late and been a long day. Let's go to bed. The officer promised to call when they learn more. The story should be on the news and the missing persons alert should be out, so perhaps we'll hear something tomorrow. How will I ever explain this to everyone?"

"Maybe you should try being honest for once. I'm sleeping in Johnny's room tonight."

#

The night is long and lonely. I go over the facts several times. The sun rises and I go into the kitchen for coffee. Margaret is there sitting with a cup.

"Did you sleep at all?" I ask.

"No, of course not."

The phone rings, and we jump.

"Hello, this is Robert Westwood."

"Mr. Westwood, my name is Eric Snyder, and I am an Associated Press reporter in St Louis. I read the missing persons notice about your boy. If you would be willing, I'd like to interview you.

"Mr. Westwood, this must be a terrible time. I want to help. What I write will be read by many media outlets, and the news about your son will reach just about everywhere. It is quite a story. I interviewed the officer in Cairo, and he told me most of it. I want to rest from you. What do you say?"

"Do you think your story will help us find Johnny?"

"Please don't take this the wrong way. I mean to be helpful. If Johnny is still alive, surely this story will find him."

I pause and think. I hear Margaret's words about being honest in my head. I want to change, but can I admit to the world that my son has run away because of me?

I don't have a choice; I'm either honest, or I lose my son.

"Ok, come anytime sooner the better."

"I'm in St. Louis. I'll leave now, should be there in about three hours. Thank you, Mr. Westwood. It'll be helpful if you could share some photos when I'm there."

Margaret starts cleaning the house as we anxiously await the reporter. I take out my map and study it once again.

South, north, east, or west? Maybe he would go somewhere familiar?

I think about the places we have gone and focus on Colorado. He enjoyed the trip there. If Johnny was brave enough to float down the Mississippi, he might try to make his way back to Colorado. On the other hand, he may continue to go South to the Gulf Coast because we once spent time near Gulfport. He loved the beaches, made sandcastles, and waded out as far as he could.

Margaret sits down beside me and looks over at the map. She agrees these two directions seem the most likely, given he loved both places.

"Robert, what do you want me to tell people?"

"I agree with what you said last night; I need to be honest if we are to bring him back. I'm through drinking. I'm done caring what anyone but you and Johnny think. I want our son back."

I walk to the liquor cabinet and take out as many bottles as I can hold into the kitchen. I open the first bottle and pour it down the drain. I take a deep breath and open the next, planning to do the same. Margaret walks in and stops me.

"We have lost our son. I'll do anything to have him back."

I pour the remaining bottles on the cabinet down the drain and walk back to the cabinet for more.

Margaret stares at me in silence.

"I'm through with the stuff."

She shakes her head and remains silent.

"We must be honest with the Associated Press reporter. I think what he writes and how far it reaches will make a huge difference in whether we bring Johnny back or not. I don't care what the local folks and our friends think. I'm going to be a good father from now on. I hope it is not too late. My God, Maggie, he is our only child!"

I feel the tears running down my cheek and bury my head in my hands, crying. I can't stop it.

"I'll stop drinking with you, Robert, I promise. I hope we can keep it up, change our lives, find Johnny, and be a happy family."

We sit and wait nervously for the AP writer to arrive. Sitting here doing nothing is not accomplishing anything. Suddenly, the doorbell rings. Eric Snyder introduces himself and I invite him in. We sit in the living room and begin to share our story. He's a good listener and is here to help. I tell him everything we suspect.

"Thank you for sharing your story so honestly, Mr. Westwood. With your permission, I will write this up and send it to my editor. The editor will decide how far to send the story."

"Absolutely."

"This story will be published in every major newspaper and will appear on television broadcasts and radio stations across the county. I've gotta ask you, are you prepared for that?"

"Yes! Anything to have Johnny back."

Chapter 8

I notice that after finishing his sandwich, my seatmate is already fast asleep.

I'm on my way to Denver!

I can't believe it. I clean up the crumbs around me and climb over Jim to take out my atlas from my bag and study it. We will go across the state of Missouri on I-70 and continue across Kansas to Colorado and then the rest of the way into Denver. Pretty simple. I lean against the window using a blanket and shut my eyes. I'm on my way to an unknown future. I feel lucky I met Waldo. If I need help, I can call him.

I hear babies crying in the back of the bus. People are reading magazines and newspapers.

What if my escape gets in the newspaper? Or on TV? Worse, the

Internet?

I suppose a missing boy lost and a raft broken to pieces would attract a lot of attention.

I need to change my appearance.

I'll shave my head and purchase a Broncos cap when we arrive in Denver. A razor can't cost much.

I managed to sleep past midnight, but now I need to go to the bathroom. Jim is still fast asleep. The babies have quit crying. I manage to climb over Jim without waking him. I make my way to the back of the bus using the seats to keep from stepping on feet that stretch across the aisle. I enter the small chamber, and to my surprise, it's pretty clean. A young man with a "Breckenridge Ski Resort" t-shirt is sitting across from the door to the bathroom. He is wide awake and nods to me as I step out.

"Are you going up to one of the ski resorts from Denver?"

"Why, yes, I am. Are you going up to the mountains too?"

"Yes, I hope to find a summer job."

He motions for me to sit down in the empty seat next to him and says, "I'm Bradley; what's your name?"

"I'm Jimmy; nice to meet you, Bradley."

"I work in Breckenridge during the summers to help me pay my college tuition. I go to Washington University in St. Louis."

"What kind of summer work are you wanting?"

"I was hoping you might give me some ideas."

"I drive a small tour bus up the ski roads that cross the mountain and eventually end up at the top. I could ask my company, Breckenridge Mountain Tours if they could use a young guy like you. They are great to work for. Would you like for me to do that?"

I wish I had an ID!

"How are you going to get to Breckenridge?" I ask.

"My girlfriend is picking me up. We met last summer and have been staying in touch. She sells tickets for the tours. Her name is Susan. Do you want to ride up with us?"

"Awesome. How can I thank you?"

"Jimmy, nice to meet you; we'll go together when we arrive in Denver; you'll like Susan. Call me Brad."

"Thanks, Brad."

I climb over more outstretched feet. Jim doesn't move as I climb into my seat. I watch the Kansas towns pass by in the moonlight.

#

I'm so excited about getting a ride to the mountains and making new friends. Brad and Susan can tell me where I can find a hostel. I turn to Jim, whose eyes have opened, and share the good news. He smiles.

"You certainly have had a good stroke of luck, young man. You can find a job where all those rich folks spend their money, and you'll do OK."

"Can you think of anything those folks might pay me directly for rather than working for someone else?"

"Most do not mow their grass, which is always the first thought I have. You could promote yourself as a set of helping hands willing to do anything. Carry luggage and groceries for people, wash and detail their cars, things like that. Rich people don't like to work if they are on vacation—so making things easy might be profitable."

He says this with such confidence I believe him. I settle back in my seat and imagine being my boss and helping in many ways. Before I know it, I'm asleep.

I wake to Jim shaking my shoulder. Bright sunlight is pouring through the windows of the bus as it slows to a stop in front of a large diner connected to a truck stop full of eighteen-wheelers. I think of Waldo as I follow nearly all of the passengers to the front door. I make a mental note to call him or find a place to send him an email to tell him about Brad, his girlfriend, and the ski resort called Breckenridge. Jim has told me that we are stopping for a snack, gas, and a stretch.

I stand aside, waiting for Brad to appear. He jumps over the last step to the ground and walks right up to me.

"Hey, buddy, let's go grab something to eat." He motions for me to follow him and we grab some milk and donuts. At the checkout, I realized I left my money pouch on the bus. I freeze.

"My money, it's on the bus, Brad; I've got to go get it."

"Don't worry, Jimmy, I'll pay for this, and you can buy the next round of goodies when we arrive in Denver."

"Do you think my money is safe?"

"Sure, no one is going to go through your stuff on this bus."

We sit down and we eat fast using all the 20 minutes. "The man sitting next to me on the bus tells me I could probably find cash work and make more; what do you think? Would people pay for things like carrying bags from the parking lots or washing and detailing cars?"

"That's a possibility, but why would you rather work for yourself for cash?"

"Cash is king! No taxes, no reporting, seems like I'd make more."

"If it works. Otherwise, you won't make anything. I need more security."

"Are there any hostels where I might stay?"

"There are two, but one of them is a long walk to downtown. They fill up quickly, but you may be lucky. Susan and I stay with other college students in one of the less expensive motels. We have a four-bedroom suite. Four sofas fold out into beds. If you can't find a place, we could probably let you hang out on one of the sofas until the better hostel has an opening. Our friends who share the cost are great people; I'm sure they will be OK with the arrangement. You can buy everyone a treat now and then to show your gratitude."

We walk back on the bus, and I see this young man going through my bag where my wallet is.

"WHAT ARE YOU DOING IN MY BAG?"

Brad then yells, "Get out of his things and hand over the wallet!"

The man looks around and is trapped because I'm in front of him, and Brad is behind me, so he can't escape off the bus without us moving.

"HERE then."

He throws the wallet at me. And pushes toward me so I'll let him off.

"Jimmy, check to make sure it's all there before we let him off."

I look and all the money and Waldo's number are there.

"It's there, let him go."

We step aside, and he gets off the bus. I didn't recognize him; I think he got on to rob people. Waldo was right; I must be more careful. I'd been in trouble if we would have been any later. The bus driver was not on the bus, so anyone could have entered. Lesson learned.

Jim gets on, and I tell him what happened.

"You have to be careful, Jimmy. I saw you eating with that other young man; it sounds like he was helpful when you had to confront that man. Seems you have someone looking out for you, Jimmy."

"Yes, I do!"

My excitement and fear are at an all-time high. I had no idea that running away from home would work out like this. I'm not sure what I expected. Growing up in my home, I learned to distrust people, especially men. I'm usually cautious. It took a long time before Mr. Olson and I became friends. Why I have taken to Brad, and Waldo too, I'm not sure. There is something about how they talk to me. I hope I've chosen to trust the right people. I don't have much of a choice. I must be more careful with my things.

As we inch closer to Denver, the land is less flat, and over long distances, I can see the landscape moving up and down.

Noticing I'm watching out the window, Jim says, "They call these the 'foothills.' We're rising to the taller mountain range, and if you try to sense it, you can feel the road climbing higher and higher in altitude. When we arrive in Denver, we'll be a mile high."

"A mile high! That's exciting."

"It is a beautiful city; I'll be visiting my grandson."

I can see he is reflecting on his upcoming visit. I'm embarrassed that I have not asked him about his life. I guess I didn't want to raise any questions about my situation.

"He's a great kid, he turns 16 tomorrow."

"Wow, old enough to drive a car."

"Maybe old enough, but that is still a ways off. He doesn't have the money. He works in a restaurant, waiting tables, and is saving his money."

We arrive at the station, and I say goodbye to Jim. I'm truly grateful and remain amazed at my streak of good luck. I see Brad getting his bags at the end of the bus and join him.

#

"OK, chap, it's time to rock and roll," Brad says cheerfully. "Let's go find Susan."

I follow along, and before I go far, I hear this joyful scream as Brad crashes into me. Someone jumps on his back. Susan is hanging on his back, kissing his neck. She had been hiding behind the side of the building.

"Susan, this is my new friend Jimmy. Jimmy is on his way to Breck to find a job and stay for the summer. Do you think we have room in your car to give him a lift?"

"Sure, plenty of room. Hey, Jimmy, I hope you like dogs, because I've brought Ginger with me to the big city. She will love you. Warning: whether you like it or not, she will try to sit in your lap."

"I love dogs."

"Yeah, well, this is one large Golden Labrador Retriever. We all take care of her; she is our mascot, protector, and friend. Will you be staying with our gang, Jimmy?"

Before I can answer, Brad chimes in, "He's looking for a spot in the local hostel. I told him about the best one and that he could stay with us until a room opens up. Do you think that will be OK with everyone?"

Susan hesitates to answer, a clue to me that it's best if I book a room as soon as I can. "That ought to work," she says, but I'm not convinced.

We hop into the car, a Volkswagen six-passenger bus. It is the old kind that hippies like my Dad used to drive around. I've seen them in lots of pictures, but I've not seen too many on the road these days. Ginger is big, no doubt about it. Her tongue leaps to my face as I climb into the middle seat. There is just enough room for the two of us. She continues to shower me with kisses.

Susan tries to calm her down but isn't successful. Susan then turns her attention instead to Brad. They have missed each other. They talk non-stop until we are clear of Denver and going up a long, steep incline that lifts us out of the valley into the mountains. The Volkswagen's engine is not strong, and we creep up the hills.

Brad pulls over into the far lane along with trucks that are also struggling with the climb. Once to the top, we sail down the other side only to encounter still another challenge as we move further and further into the mountain range.

Breckinridge is a cute little community nestled between mountains. I can see cutouts of trees in the mountains. I suspect they are ski runs. I try to imagine what they must look like with snow on them. I'm nervous, not certain what will happen next.

"Jimmy, I think I'll take you by the hostel right now to see if you can book a room sooner the better."

The hostel is a couple of blocks off the main strip of the town on the side opposite the ski runs. It looks pretty much like all the other houses, and there is no name or marking on the front. Brad motions for me to join him while Becca waits. Just inside, a young man and woman are walking out. Brad says hello and asks about rooms.

"Hi, I'm Brad McGraw, and this is my friend Jimmy, who is looking for a room. Are any available?"

"I think there will be one available later today. It's down at the end of the hall. Alison is still here and could probably tell you if Joe and Sharon have rented it. I'm sure she'll talk to you; she got back from an early lunch."

It appears that all the people living here have met. Joe and Sharon must be the owners. We walk down the hall, knock on the door, and an attractive young woman greets us.

"Hi, looking for a room?"

"You must be Allison?"

"These rooms are popular, so they don't stay empty long. When I told Mary, the manager, I was leaving, she told me to let her know if others were looking for a room. I was getting ready to call her on my cell phone. What are your names?"

Brad explains that the room is for me and that I hope to stay for the summer.

"The name is Jimmy Olson."

"Like the guy in *Superman*?"

"Yes, but he's no Superman."

Hope she doesn't ask my age or for ID.

She begins to punch in a number, and I can tell from the conversation that I'm going to book the room.

"It is $20 a night." I nod my head once again, and before I know it, she hands the phone to me.

"It's Mary on the line."

Mary explains some of the rules that seem simple enough to me. I provide everything: sheets, linens, towels, keep the place clean, no parties, no drinking alcohol or any other drugs, eat my meals out, leave no crumbs from snacks, toilet at the end of the hall, and make no noise. I promise to leave $100 for the first five days in a box at the front door as directed.

I drop my stuff off in the room, walk to Walmart a few doors down, and pick up a pair of scissors, a hat, and a razor so I can shave my head. Allison and that young couple are the only ones who saw me, and Allison is leaving. I can't afford for anyone else to see me, or they will wonder why I'm shaving my head. I head back to my room and begin cutting my hair as close as I can and then shaving it.

Goodbye, Johnny. Hello, Jimmy.

I wish I would have thought of this sooner, but I should still be OK. I put on my ball cap, clean up my mess, and head down the hall to the living room.

#

I'm watching the news with another young man and woman, and suddenly there is a photo of me on the TV! I'm shocked by the story and only hear the newsman's final remarks.

"If you see this young man, please call the authorities or Mr. Eric Smith of the *St Louis Post Dispatch*. There is a reward for information leading to his whereabouts."

OH NO! I hope those two weren't paying attention and didn't notice me! I've got to escape out of here!

I quietly rise and head back to my room so I can think.

Brad and Susan of course, saw me and talked with me; they were too busy to watch TV.

What should I do?

I need to escape out of town, as someone may have recognized me. I need to find a place where I can blend in and hide. I'm glad I haven't unpacked my things! I grab the backpack and check the hallway to make sure it is clear. I see the "rent box" and decide it's fair if I pay one night's rent. I pry open the box and take out my envelope with the $100. I leave $20 and take the $80. I leave the other envelopes in the box. It's my money, and I'm leaving. Joe and Sharon will appreciate that I leave one night's stay. I don't bother to put a note.

I exit the hostel and go to pick up a shuttle. I think I'm in the right place, but I'm not certain as I didn't see a sign. I see a police car drive by, and I simply turn my back to the road and look up into the mountains like so many other people in town. The car moves down the street.

Time goes so slowly when you are in a hurry. It seems like hours before the first shuttle arrives, but it was only 15 or 20 minutes. I climb on the bus, discover it is going to Vail over the next mountain pass, and settle in a seat in the back. The shuttle is free, but I still don't know what to do.

Should I go on to the next resort?

What about riding this bus all day?

I think of Waldo, and now James, who most likely turned me in. It's then that I notice a copy of *USA Today* sitting on the seat across from me. I can't believe my eyes when I see my picture on the front page. I grab the paper and turn to the inside story, and there it is: the story of my escape down the Mississippi River on a homemade raft, the remnants found on a sandbar, and the belief that I'm still alive but on

84

the run. I read with great interest that the rope tying the logs together had been cut.

Darn, they figured it out.

I quickly stuff the paper in my jeans pocket and look out the window. We arrive in Vail much too fast, and I hurriedly jump off the shuttle and make sure that I'm not in the direct vision of tourists and others. I walk to the edge of the mountain, where a small creek passes by. There is an asphalt path along the stream, and I find a secluded bench. It is there I begin to plan my next move.

Where can I go, hide? Hiding is nothing new to me, but doing it in unfamiliar territory is another matter. I once again pull out my Atlas and explore possibilities. I have no idea where to run. I see a hotel and think it might have one of those racks with tourist attractions. I cautiously approach the entrance and slip into the front lobby.

There, it is over in a corner. I walk to it and begin picking out every brochure, map, and other advertisement. I've quite a collection. I put half of them into my clothes bag and return to my special bench beside the running water. I begin to study each one.

"So where are you going, young man?"

The words come over my shoulder, and I jump what seems like five feet into the air. I think I let out a little scream at the same time.

An older, kind-looking man is peering down at me and apologizing for frightening me.

"I'm sorry. I didn't mean to startle you. I saw you looking at all those attractions and wondered what caught your fancy."

I am so relieved that he doesn't recognize me as the runaway kid from Missouri. More importantly, I like him. He's gentle and seems genuinely interested in my plans. I suspect he is about 30 or 40 years old.

"I don't know. I've no transportation, so it is going to be hard to go to any of these places."

"I have a car; perhaps I can take you. Where would you like to go?"

"I love the Rocky Mountain National Park, but it is a long way."

"Well, what a coincidence. I'm driving to Estes Park this afternoon; would you like a ride?"

"Oh, yes. That would be so kind of you."

"I'll meet you at the place up there where all the buses stop. Be there around 2 p.m. I'm looking forward to having someone to talk to on the way. By the way, my name is Paul; what's yours?"

"Jimmy Olson. See you at 2."

#

I wait patiently for 2 p.m. to roll around. Although hungry, I don't dare go to a restaurant where I might be recognized. Most of all, I am praying that Paul is not aware of who he will be taking to Estes Park. Hopefully, he doesn't read USA Today or watch the news. Paul drives up in a car, but as I reach for the door handle, I see there is a police car three cars back.

I think he has turned me in! I turn and run as fast as I can down the steps and into a crowd of people. I slow down and try to blend into the group. Another group of kids my age is coming in the opposite direction, and I silently move into that group to better hide. I look around, and no one is coming, so I start to feel safe. I see no sign of Paul or any policemen. I either got away, or I was mistaken and missed a chance for a ride.

I want to go to Estes Park, but how can I find safe transportation there? I walk with the group and think about a plan. I remember what Waldo said about being careful and not trusting everyone off the bat. I made that mistake with Paul, I'm sure. But if I can't trust getting a ride with someone, how will I get to Estes?

I see an isolated bench again and sit down to think. It's facing the stream rather than the path everyone is walking on, so no one can see my face. Suddenly, an older man sits down next to me.

"Mind if I sit here? I need a break. It's been a long and emotional day for me. My name is Fred."

"Hi, Fred. I'm Jimmy. I've also had a long day. I'm trying to solve a problem and not having a lot of luck."

"What's the problem, young man? I'm a good problem solver."

"I need to find a way to Estes Park so I can hike in Rocky Mountain National Park. My Dad and I did it a few years ago and I'm excited to try by myself and relive those memories."

"You're in luck. I'm heading that way as soon as I rest. I'd love some company if you want to join me."

If we leave now, I know he can't turn me in before we go. This older man must be safe. I haven't got much choice. It is either take my chances with him or go back to my family. Dad would no doubt beat me for embarrassing him. I can only imagine the lies they're telling their friends about my disappearance. They probably said I was an adventurous person and loved taking risks. I can hear my Dad holding forth, gathering a large audience. He's probably saying things like, "A chip off the old block, that's my boy! Rafting down the Mississippi, what a daring yet unsafe thing to do." And all that nonsense in the newspaper article about loving me and desperately wanting to find me and bring me home. It's all bullshit.

"I'd appreciate it. Just let me know when you are ready to go; I'm ready anytime.

"I'm parked in the lot up the stairs behind us. I'm ready, let's head out."

My heart is racing, and I can feel it pounding in my chest. These and other thoughts send my imagination swimming. I cross my fingers and follow.

We approach the car, a big black Lincoln Town Car; oh my God, this guy is rich. He unlocks the door, gets in, and motions for me to get in. I slide in, clothes bag and all.

"Hi, Jimmy. Are you ready to go over the mountains?"

"Fred, I'm as ready as I'll ever be."

I feel kind of sensitive about calling an older man by his first name. I think he realizes this and says, "If you are wondering, my last name is Zweig, but please keep calling me Fred. I like that."

"I hope to find a job to help me save money to go to college next year.

Vail is expensive. I hope to find something near the National Park. I love the Rocky Mountains. And what do you do, Mr. Zweig? I mean, Fred?"

"I am retired, Jimmy. My wife died earlier this year, and I'm driving to all our favorite spots. A kind of farewell tour. I'm hoping it will help me grieve." Watching him reflect as he searches his memories, a period of silence ensues.

"She was a beautiful woman, Jimmy. I loved her very much. We did everything together. She would love to meet a young man like you. She'd tell you about hiking in these mountains, camping out in the park, bringing our children here, and more. Estes was our favorite place to visit. Our favorite place was a hotel called The Craig's. It's one of the oldest hotels and is still there on the side of a mountain overlooking the town. I'd be glad to show it to you; I'm planning to spend a couple of days there."

"I'm sorry she died."

"So where are you staying tonight, Jimmy? Do you have some friends in Estes?"

"No, no friends. I hope to find a hostel."

"I don't know of any hostel in Estes Park, but I guess there may be one. We will ask at The Craig's when we arrive."

"That would be great, Fred; I don't know how to thank you."

"Ah, no problem, I've nothing else to do. Do you live in Colorado or somewhere else?"

"Missouri. I live in St. Louis, Missouri. I plan to go to Washington

University. My Dad is a lawyer and insists that I contribute to the cost of tuition by getting a summer job. The idea to come to Colorado was mine. I'm not sure if I'll make a dent in the tuition if I don't find a job soon."

"Undoubtedly, you will find something in Estes Park. I'm friends with the owners of the Craig's, they could use a young man like you. Why don't we go there first and see what might be possible?"

If only I had an ID, that would work. How do I respond?

"Wow, Fred, that would be great! I guess there's nothing to lose in asking; thanks so much!"

I'll deal with it if anything comes of it.

"Sounds like a plan to me."

As we cross Trail Ridge Road, we talk about the wildlife in the Park, the beauty of the mountains, and the changing seasons. It is a comfortable conversation; I feel like I'm back home talking with Mr. Olson on his front porch.

Thanks to the front desk at The Craig's, I found the hostel, and they have an opening. The manager was also named Mary, and she gave me rent for $15 a night. I paid for only one night. Fred didn't see the person he knew, so there were no issues with the job. I settled in for the night and fell asleep. I'm at least safe for now.

Chapter 9

"Mr. Westwood, we have a report on a young man meeting Johnny's description. I wanted you to know right away."

"Thank you, officer. What do we know?"

"We have a report he was seen in Breckenridge, Colorado."

"I've been thinking, and we had a trip to Colorado that he enjoyed, so I was wondering if that might be somewhere he would go."

"We don't know for sure it was him, so try not to set your hopes too high."

"What is the next step, officer?"

"We will ask the local authorities to try and find him and obtain some more information."

"I'll be there in 12 hours. Just say the word?"

"Stay put for now. I hope to hear something in the next couple of hours."

"Ok, officer. I look forward to your call!"

I should start driving toward Colorado.

I hang up the phone and turn to Margaret with tears in my eyes.

"Someone has seen him and called! They had a report in Breckinridge, Colorado."

Margaret smiles and states, "He's alive, he's alive, he's alive!"

"Stay calm as we aren't 100% sure yet."

We are both staring at the telephone, holding our breath, waiting for it to ring. As if the phone felt our anxiety, it rings, and we both jump up to grab it.

"Robert, it is Eric Snyder. I think I have good news."

"Yes, Eric, please tell me everything."

"I received a call from someone at a youth hostel in Breckinridge, Colorado. A young woman told me she believes someone is staying there that may be Johnny, although he has shaved his head."

"Eric, that is fantastic. I can be there in 12 hours. I'm packed and ready to go."

"Hold on for a little bit. She's going to try and snap a photo and send it to me so we can make sure. You don't want to head west only to find a new report that he went south."

"I suppose that makes sense, but I also don't want to waste a minute.

I'll be patient a bit longer."

"The woman's name is Judy and she said he left this morning headed to town for something. She said she'll watch for his return and use discretion to take a photo. She's motivated by the reward and understands we don't want him to suspect anything and run off."

As soon as I hang up the phone, it rings again. At the same time, my email is also going crazy with new messages. Seems like everyone who read the news or watched TV now knows about the "rafting kid" who has run away from home. People are calling for more information or to offer their support. I'm so surprised that people are reaching out instead of being critical and questioning my parenting.

While I'm waiting for a confirmation call from the reporter, I decide to check on flights to Denver, so I'll know what all the options are. We have no airport of any size in Cape, so I'll have to drive to St. Louis, which is a two-hour drive. There are four nonstop flights out of St Louis, so I can make one of them quickly.

Two hours later, I got a call from Eric. He emails a photo of a shaved head and a hat. I recognize his smile. I show the photo to Margaret, and we both yell out loud. She makes the call to buy my tickets as I grab my bag and head out the door. She is going to stay home in case he happens to call, or any new information comes in.

I have several pictures of Johnny in my luggage. Eric notified the police, who have agreed to keep an eye on the hostel but not approach Johnny to scare him away.

I arrive in Denver, rent a car, and drive to Breckenridge. I stop in at the local police office to check in and develop a plan. Jim Ross is the officer assigned to the case. We agree that I'd wait in the car while he goes to the hostel to investigate more closely.

"Mr. Westwood, we need to be careful not to alert him that we know who he is. We don't want him running off."

"I agree, officer. I'll trust you on this and wait patiently so as not to scare him away."

I ride in the squad car with Officer Ross and wait as he enters the hostel. I struggle to breathe as I wait to see Johnny come out of the door with the officer. I also watch the building carefully to ensure he doesn't run off. After 20 minutes, I see the uniformed man exit the building and head back to the car.

"Bad news, Mr. Westwood. It appears Johnny knew we had been contacted and left. His things are missing from the room. The lock box with the rental payments was pried open. The manager believes he got into the envelope with his name and took back his deposit, leaving payment only for one night. No other funds are missing."

My heart sinks. I thought we had found him.

"When was this? Do we have any idea where he went?"

"He left without a word to anyone at the hostel. We aren't even sure of the exact time he left. Since he left a one-night payment, I assume he spent one night, which was three days ago. We will now contact the bus shuttle company and see if anyone has seen him, and perhaps we will have a clue. I suggest you find a hotel for tonight, and let's see what I can turn up this afternoon."

Another dead end.

I wake to a call from Officer Ross.

"Robert, we have a new lead. It may not be anything, but one of the bus drivers gave him a ride into Vail. He had a backpack with him. That was in the afternoon two days ago. We are getting close."

"Thank you, officer. What can I do?"

"I've contacted the Vail Police, and it's now in their hands. I suggest you head over there."

"I'll leave right now and check in at the station."

I pack my things and check out of the hotel, hoping I can find a lead and chase it. I arrive in Vail and check into another hotel. The Vail Police have no leads at this time. They suggest I show his picture around and see if anything turns up. I take a copy of the most recent photo and stand on the corner of the main street through town. As people come to the crossing, I show them the photo and ask if they have seen him. I know it's a long shot.

A teenage girl about Johnny's age walks by, and I approach her with the photo stretched out toward her.

"Have you seen, by chance, this young man in the last couple of days?"

She looks and says, "Yes, I saw him a couple of days ago getting off a bus. He looked lost. He headed toward that hotel." She points at the hotel a couple of blocks over.

"Here is my business card. If you think of anything else, please call me. We are desperate to find him. It appears I missed him."

"Ok, no problem."

"Thanks."

I call Margaret with the news about Vail, Colorado.

#

I go directly to the station and meet the Police Chief, Les Hall. I start to speak and my voice quivers. I fight back tears.

"Officer Hall, have you heard anything about Johnny's possible whereabouts? Anything new? I met a young lady who identified him from the photo and said she saw him get off the bus."

"I can almost guarantee you that if he is in Vail, we will find him. Every hotel, restaurant, bus service, and all of our officers have been alerted and are on the lookout for him."

"I'll be staying at the Marriott Streamside on the West end. Is it OK with you that I plan to walk around town looking for him? I won't disturb anyone. I'll show people Johnny's picture and ask if they've seen him. Is that OK?"

"Of course."

#

I check in to the hotel and unpack. I walk along an asphalt walking path by a creek, making my way into the heart of town. Now and then, I see another pedestrian hiking the path and show them Johnny's picture. I grow tired and see a secluded bench and sit down to rest. I need some space. I look down at the ground and see a brochure of some kind. I lean over and pick it up.

"Visit Bear Lake, the heart of the Rocky Mountain National Park."

If I wanted to hide and was running, I'd head to the park. Johnny has been there before and loved it. I bet he's heading there!

Knowing it's just a hunch, I don't mention it to Officer Hall or even to Margaret. I'll give Vail a couple of days. It seems so logical, and Johnny has made decisions based on his experience all along this journey.

I reflect on trying to understand how we managed to end up in this place. My career has driven everything. I was so concerned about my success that I'd forgotten about my son. I work so many late nights. We have social events every weekend. We've skipped vacation for the past couple of years. If life is exhausting for me, what must it have all been for Johnny?

I've been such a bad father. I swore I wouldn't be like my dad, and look at me. I like the parties and the alcohol. I love being the life of all parties. I enjoy being the first to arrive so I can meet people as they come in. I also like to be the last to leave so I don't miss anything.

I know I sometimes have a bit too much and that I then become impatient at home. My temper has gotten the better part of me a couple of times. I fight back the tears of regret.

If I have another chance, I'll make it all up to both Margaret and Johnny.

Two days later, there is still no sign of Johnny. I contact Officer Hall again.

"We think he must have left town, Robert."

"I think he may have gone to Rocky Mountain National Park. We spent some time there a couple of years ago, and he loved it. The more I think about it, the more logical it is that he would somehow make his way there."

"I'll alert all the Park Rangers and all the establishments in Estes Park. And don't worry, we'll continue to keep our eyes open around here for Johnny."

"Thank you so much, Officer. This may be a lost cause, but I must keep looking."

"Good luck, Robert."

#

If I'm right and Johnny is in Estes Park, I lost three precious days in Vail, Colorado. On the way to Estes Park, I call Margaret to give her an update.

"I've decided to go on to Estes Park. I have a feeling that is where Johnny went. I'll contact both the local authorities and the US Park Service. I'm also going to distribute the photos and try to put up flyers while I'm there."

"There was no sign of him in Vail?"

"Nothing other than confirmation from a young woman he got off the bus. Everything in me is pointing to Estes Park."

"I agree. He loved it so much there. He even has that poster on the wall in his room."

"I'll call you in a couple of days with an update. Maggie, I love you; please don't give up hope. We need to stay positive."

"Robert, I love you too. I'm trying hard to believe you will find our son."

I find a hotel with a vacancy. Nearly every hotel in the area is occupied, as it is peak season. I unpack and grab a stack of bulletins and my photo to see what I can stir up. The park is huge with few rangers, so it would be a perfect place to hide. I go first to the local police and explain who I am and how they can reach me. I then go to the park officers and provide the same information.

Exhausted, I head into the town of Estes Park and buy hiking boots, jeans, a sweatshirt and coat, a backpack, and a few other items. I decide I'm hiking up to The Loch in case he remembered. On the way back, I look up into the mountains and see it snowing at the peaks.

For a moment, I begin to think I'm crazy for doing this. Then I remember this was the same boy who built a raft and floated down the Mississippi River. For a second, I'm proud, the next angry, and the next sad.

I head to the nearest liquor store; I need a drink. I go inside and grab a bottle of vodka. I hold it in my hand. I head to the counter, and the man puts the bottle in a sack. I arrive at the motel and head into the bathroom to grab a cup. I open the bottle and smell it.

Just this one time. I need a drink to help process all this. No one will ever know. I deserve this after all I've been through getting here.

I pour half a glass and take it to the chair and small table. Three times,

I raise the glass to my lips. All this stress could soon evaporate, at least for a while. What is stopping me?

If I take a drink, I break my promise to myself and Margaret. I should drink this bottle and head right back home to Cape Girardeau. The police need to do their job. I'm wasting my time.

I start shaking.

What should I do?

What's more important? This drink or Johnny?

"No, no, no!"

I slam the glass down so hard that the vodka splashes everywhere. I walk over to the bathroom, grab a towel, and walk to the table to wipe up the spilled poison. I then grab the bottle and quickly return to the bathroom and pour every drop down the drain. I sit down on the floor next to the stool, close the lid, and cry as hard as I ever cried. I wake up next to the stool in the bathroom.

I'm happy I made the right choice. Johnny is much more important than that one bottle of vodka. If only my dad had made that choice even one time. I'm not going to be like my dad. I want Johnny home, and I want him to love me. Even if Johnny isn't in the mountains and is never found, I want to stop drinking. I'm going to find that Alcoholics Anonymous group and find help. I call Margaret.

"Maggie, I'm going hiking in the mountains to look for him."

"It's 5 a.m. What are you doing up, Robert?"

"I've been doing a lot of thinking; I will share it with you when we are together again."

"Have you been drinking, Robert?"

"No, I haven't. I'm going to keep looking for Johnny until I find him, Maggie. Don't worry, I haven't had a drink. I'm stopping."

"Go to the Loch," she says hurriedly, tears in her voice. "He'll go there; he always talks about it, even after all these years!"

"OK, I'll try there first; don't worry about me."

Chapter 10

I rest well at the hostel and sleep till 7 a.m. I shower and pack my bag. I'm going to hike up to The Loch. I head out the door and run into Fred. He asks me if I'd like to go to breakfast with him at the place next door. I agree that a hot meal would help me hike.

"Hi, Jimmy. Have a seat; the breakfast here is delicious. Glad to see you up and early."

I order two eggs over-easy, white toast, bacon, and three fluffy pancakes. To this, I order orange juice and a tall glass of milk to wash it down.

"Well, young man, will you now please tell me more about yourself?"

What do I want to tell him? I didn't expect that question.

"Yes, I want to share all of it with you, Fred, but I have one favor to ask. Would it be possible for you to take and drop me off at the entrance to Rocky Mountain National Park? I want to hike up one of the trails and enjoy the scenery. I was here when I was much younger, and I want to experience it again. How about we meet tonight after my hike?"

"Sure, Jimmy. You can call me on my cell phone when you are ready to return. Here is a prepaid cell phone for you. I'll come pick you up at the entrance or wherever you wish."

I can tell by his excitement that he suspects nothing. He is glad that I haven't run away and will be joining him for dinner. I write down his phone number and stick it and the phone in my bag with the notes for my great escape. At the end of the day, I'll call him and tell him not to worry that I caught a ride in the Park back to St. Louis. I'll say that I was running away, and it was time to return home. He should be happy about that. I'll add that meeting him made me decide to stop running.

I feel kind of guilty for duping him, but in a way, his innocence in all of this should protect him once the truth is revealed. He'll realize that I didn't want him to be caught assisting a teenage runaway.

We leave the hotel at about 9 a.m., and Fred drives me to Bear Lake. He tells me all the good trails in the park take off from there. The traffic is thick, and although the shuttles are already running, he drops me off. He pats me on the back as I exit the car.

"See you later, Jimmy. Enjoy yourself."

"I will, Fred. Expect to receive a call late this afternoon, most likely when the sun is going down."

Many people are emerging from their cars in all kinds of hiking gear.

Some are carrying large coolers full of picnic supplies, and others are simply there for a short walk around the lake. I find a map and sit on a bench, studying the various trails for a long while. I see The Loch on the map. I need some safe space to think about what I'm going to do. That trail has many forks along the path, and anyone trying to follow or find me would have difficulty knowing where to turn or where to look. I should be safe up there as long as my food holds out. I remember that you can drink the water from the small streams high in the mountains; it's not yet contaminated by its long flow to the ocean.

Tightening my tennis shoes, I begin my trek toward Glacier Gorge Junction and then up the trail to a series of waterfalls about one mile distant. There, I plan to catch my breath for what appears to be a long climb up the mountain. It is sunny and about 75 degrees.

The trees against the crystal clear blue sky are spectacular. I encounter many hikers early in the climb. They range from families with children to young and old couples. I'm the only hiker who is alone.

Everyone is friendly, waving and sharing warm greetings as I pass by. You can go much faster by yourself, not having to wait for others. The altitude will eventually approach two miles when I reach the timberline, requiring more rest along the way.

My early first stop is the waterfall. I find many hikers spread out on rocks beside the rushing water that borders a long section of the path. Others are so out of breath, especially the older ones, that this is as far as they go. Many are turning around to go down the mountain instead of up it. Fred had graciously stopped at a grocery store, so I had plenty of goodies to snack on. I use this opportunity to eat a Snickers bar.

I estimate that about two hours later, after many rest stops and turns in the path, I finally reach The Loch. Nestled in the arms of several mountains, the lake is like a mirror. I walk over a large outcropping of boulders, and I see the full lake spread out before me.

A young boy has thrown a rock into the quiet, still waters, and the concentric circles are fascinating to watch as they spread from their origin. I find a sunny spot, lie down, and shut my eyes, thinking about my next move.

There are too many people here. There is no question I must go higher to find quiet. I eat some cheese and crackers and decide to move on. The trail is harder to follow, but I see a sign to Looking Glass Lake, Sky Pond, and Andrew's Glacier. I am going in the right direction. I come to Timberline Falls, and the trail goes directly up the falls themselves. I am required to use rocks protruding out from beneath the falling water; it is both fun and risky.

A slip will cause a fall down a considerably steep embankment, but I make it without too much difficulty. Reaching the top I am overwhelmed looking back on The Loch and the valley cutting through the mountains. It is the most beautiful sight I have ever seen. Looking Glass Lake is ahead, and a short distance in another direction is Sky Pond. The wind is the only hindrance to an otherwise pristine setting.

I find some shelter behind a large boulder behind which there is a clump of short but sturdy trees. They seem to be the only trees at this altitude. I begin to fortify my shelter. Finding old burnt-out timber, I build a lean-to and cover it with all kinds of old limbs. When finished, I feel like I am back in my cliff cave in Cape Girardeau.

I have blocked the wind, and while I can hear it howling through the mountain peaks, I feel safe and comfortable in my new abode. I make it further habitable by digging out a space for a fire and an escape passage for the smoke and air to move through my makeshift roof and out into what will soon be a night sky.

I bring out my cell phone to see if I have a signal. No signal. I'm as isolated as anyone could be. I remember my promise to Fred to give him a call. I was going to tell him I found a ride back to St. Louis, that yes, I was running away but had decided to stop running, and that he played a major role in the decision. Now I realize this is not going to happen. If I can stand the cold, I plan to spend the night here.

Quickly, while there is still light, I look for kindling with which I can start a fire and begin to collect several old logs that are easy to snap into many pieces. I can already tell it is going to be cold tonight, and if my fire doesn't work, I'll have to hustle down the mountain, maybe in the dark, to a warmer altitude.

When I'm sure I have more than enough raw materials, I bring them in close to the small opening I have created next to the boulder that provides the greatest protection from the wind and cold. I find it easy to pull them through when needed and begin to construct my first fire; I feel like a caveman.

I'm so busy gathering wood that I don't notice the build-up of clouds overhead. Now, I can see them clearly through my narrow entrance and also through the small hole I have created for the smoke to escape from the roof. At this altitude, it can snow anytime; this is something I hadn't figured out. I hope it isn't a fatal mistake. Before that thought has rested, I see the first snowflake.

#

Starting the fire is easier than I thought. Bringing matches with me is perhaps the smartest thing I have done on this great escape. Getting the smoke to rise in a single column and out the roof is not so easy. I move the branches over about six inches and push the wall of my enclosure away from the line of smoke. It works. Like the early Anasazi, I have built my little kiva and an opening for the spirits to rise with the smoke to the heavens. I studied the Anasazi in school, and I continue to be amazed that in America we had Indians similar to the Mayans in Mexico.

The difference between Colorado versus Mexico is the snow that is beginning to fall here in large amounts. It is covering my shelter fast. Ironically, I think I'll be warmer because of it.

Exhausted, I fall asleep listening to what sounds like clumps of snow falling and accumulating on my shelter roof. I worry about the sturdiness of the structure.

I awake to almost total darkness. My fire has gone out, and the hole I created to release smoke from it is blocked with snow. It is so quiet; I can't hear a thing. It's the most eerie feeling I have ever experienced. I'm only slightly cold, but I realize I need to find more wood for a fire. I need to restore my makeshift chimney and push it out through my small crawl space entrance.

I suppose I should be scared, but right now, surviving is on my mind.

Bundling up in what clothes I brought with me, I crawl through the entrance and am relieved to discover that it is an easy task despite a foot of snow.

Snow is about a foot tall on the roof of my shelter and halfway up on all sides. I'm able to climb up the rock side, brushing off the snow as I go until I reach the top. There, I can find the chimney hole and re-establish it. The brightness of the sun hurts my eyes and there is not a cloud in the sky to block it. From the vantage point of the rock, I look around 360 degrees and am astonished at the beauty that spreads out before me. Realizing I have work to do, I feel like the astronauts must feel when they gaze out their window at Earth. I'm beginning to get cold.

The wood I have gathered for the fire is covered but dry beneath the snow. I push several branches, small and large, into the shelter. Crawling in again, I'm amazed at how fast I have the fire going again. Warmth fills the shelter, and I begin to worry that melting snow will drip through the ceiling. I eat a couple of candy bars and suck on snow located outside the entrance. It's then I realize that there is no way I can survive up here.

I was proud of the cave on the cliffs overlooking the Mississippi, but I must admit this shelter is something to behold. I wish I had a camera to record every inch and location of it. Against the dark blue sky, it looks like a mountaintop igloo somewhere in the Arctic Circle. I decided to absorb as much warmth as possible, collect my bag of clothes and remaining food, and head back down the mountain. I expect it to be warm by noon, and once below the tree line, the rest of the descent should be easier.

Summer blizzards at this high altitude are not rare, but I don't want to go through another one. Besides, dangerous animals may come out of hiding, looking for food. I don't want to be what they choose for dinner. Although an experience I never want to forget, I feel like it may have been stupid to escape to an unforgiving environment like this.

When the sun is high, I leave my sturdy shelter for the next visitor to use as needed. Each step takes extra time since the snow is deep. Along the way I wonder how long my igloo will hold together; I hope for a long time.

I reach the top of the Timberline Falls. To the left is what appears to be a smooth downhill incline, and while steep, it seems safe. Sliding on my butt, I think I can reach the trees below in record time and bypass what could be a treacherous climb down the falls. I decide to do it, and what a great decision. I almost shout out loud with glee as I slide down the mountain like a human sled.

Just before coming to the trees, I experience an abrupt stop. I think I've covered nearly one-fourth of a mile, perhaps more. I'm in the trees, along what I think is the path back to The Loch. It's also now warmer. Once at the lake, I find my favorite rocks overlooking it and lay down for a rest. The direct sunlight on my body against the warm stones is refreshing. I fall asleep.

It's a good thing I covered my head, or else I would have sunburn as bad as the one along the banks of the Mighty Mississippi. Geez, I feel like the ride down the river on my homemade raft was years ago. It's mid-afternoon, and I need a plan.

I am confident the authorities are looking for me in Estes Park and, who knows, maybe in the Rocky Mountain National Park, as well. I am a wanted man. I almost thought, "wanted boy," but this adventure is, I think, helping me think of myself as a man. I begin to tally all the stupid things I have done.

My first thought is food and water; I need both. I still have money, so I decided the next move needs to be to find a place where I can eat and be safe at the same time. I discover my jeans have dried out from the slide down the mountain. I start down the path to Bear Lake, but I'm uncertain what to do once I'm there.

Off to the side of the trail, not far from The Loch, but with a beautiful view of it, is a tent with two campers eating something over a fire. Two boys, appearing to be my age, see me looking. They motion for me to come over to their camp. I confidently head that way. It must be quite a sight.

"Hey, buddy," the tall one says, "you look exhausted and hungry. Come join us; we can't eat all these burgers."

I start to excuse myself, but the smell is overwhelming. I sit down next to the shorter one.

"Well, quite frankly, that sounds like a great idea. I'm hungry."

"So you have been hiking up there?" the tall one says as he points to almost the exact spot from which I have come. Before I can say anything, he adds, "That's where we are going tomorrow. Plan to camp out at Sky Pond."

"Yes, I built a shelter up there; feel free to use it."

I eat it like a survivor who has been lost for days.

"Do you mind if I stay the night with you guys?"

Chapter 11

The Park shuttle lets me off at Bear Lake, where the trail to The Loch begins. I see a poster board; I will show everyone my photo along the way and ask if they have seen Johnny.

Johnny, where are you?

I feel great this morning despite spending the night on the floor in the bathroom. Sober with no hangover, no remorse, no guilt feelings; I'm proud I survived the night. Determined to find my son, I'm on a mission. My family will recover from this and begin a new life.

It is early in the morning, so there aren't many people around. I walk around Bear Lake before going up the trail to The Loch.

"Good morning. Can you tell me if you have seen this young man along the trail?"

"I haven't, but I'll keep an eye out as I climb today."

"I realize you are probably getting started this morning, but have you seen this young man?"

"We came down from Alberta Falls early this morning and didn't see anything; sorry."

"I'm looking for my teenage son; can you tell me if you have seen him?"

"We are getting started; how, might I ask, does one lose a teenager? My children are small, and I certainly know when I turn my back, they are gone. I had hoped that would not be an issue as they get older?"

"I remember those days; turn your back, and they are gone. Our worries don't end when they are older; there are so many dangers, and they can make such poor decisions. As teenagers, they are so independent it can be even easier to lose them. Please keep an eye out for him, and if you see him, please let the Rangers know. Thanks."

As embarrassing as this is, as hopeless as it is, I have to do this if I have a chance of finding him. I can't let my pride be a reason not to ask.

I begin the climb to The Loch, one of three lakes in scenic Loch Vale. I can make the first five miles to Alberta Falls, where I stop and rest. I am already feeling muscles I forgot I had, and it's getting harder to breathe as I climb higher. I stop and rest.

"Have you come across this young man on the way down the mountain?"

"No, sir, it's early we have not seen anyone this morning."

I catch my breath and begin again pushing my body up the steep inclines, breathing as deeply as I can to inhale the oxygen I need. After a few minutes, I am forced again to stop and rest. I sit on a rock and memories come flooding into my tired mind.

A young couple with their son who is around 6, the same age Johnny was last time we were here, passed me while I was resting. He runs ahead and stops to look at the ground, just as Johnny did.

"Dad, give me some more trail mix to feed the chipmunks. Take this little one's picture; he is so cute. Mom, and Dad, listen to the birds; they are so loud. What kind is that?"

In contrast, the silence of today's hike is deafening.

Again, I move ahead; I feel an urgency to find him, and yet my body is fighting the journey and slowing me down. I enter the most difficult part of the trail. It is steep, near the tree line, and has a sharp drop-off on the left side of the trail.

I find a perfectly shaped flat rock to rest my aching body and catch my breath. As I recline, I put my backpack behind my head for a pillow. A beautiful blue sky with a bright sun shining off the mountain streams urged me forward.

A couple of young men are coming down the mountain, and I show them Johnny's picture.

"Did you happen to see this young man on the trail?"

"No, sir, up at the Loch, we saw a couple of young boys, but not this one."

The path near the lake becomes less distinct and difficult and rocky. I push forward, and suddenly, I hear laughter.

My heart begins racing, and I hold my breath so I can hear more clearly. It sounds like several young men having a good time. They are telling stories of some kind. I leave the trail and walk directly up the mountain toward the sounds. I can't make out what is being said. I stop as I realize I'm getting close. I'm below a large outcropping of rocks above where I think the boys are located. I strain my ears to hear what is being said.

"You built an igloo near the Andrews Glacier?"

"Yes."

Although it was only one word, I bit my lip. Oh my God, that was Johnny.

"Do you realize you could have died up there in that blizzard!" a third person stated.

"My Dad taught me how to build a shelter and how to build a fire. I did both, and believe it or not, I was comfortable up there."

I freeze. Tears fall from my eyes. Then I heard one of the boys ask, "So what is your plan, Jimmy?"

I listen carefully for the answer.

"I don't know," is the reply.

#

When I hear him say he doesn't have a plan, I don't stop to think. I rush up the mountain from behind the outcropping of rock, around a clump of trees, over a small rivulet of a stream, and right into their little gathering. I stand there facing three boys, and in the middle, is

Johnny. My instincts take over, and I yell out.

"Johnny, come home with me right now."

Johnny stands there silent. He seems terrified.

The two boys look at him at the same time.

"Is this your Dad, Jimmy?"

"YES!"

Johnny grabs his bag and bolts into the trees leading to the lake. It happens so fast; I can't react in time to catch him. I automatically dart after him. I stumble and fall. Before I can rise on two feet, I feel the grasp of arms around my ankles and circling his chest. I'm pinned on the ground by the two boys. Although bigger than either boy, I can't get free of them.

"Let me go! His name is Johnny, and he's my son!"

"Yeah, mister, Jimmy told us about you; some father you are."

"We like his new name, and so does he; why don't you leave him alone and get out of his life."

The words sink in like a knife straight through my heart. How can I convince them that I've changed?

We are spread out over the ground. I stay there and say nothing. I don't fight them. I know time is racing by with every passing minute, and Johnny is getting away. I try a new tactic.

"Please, let me go."

"You stay right there, daddy; we're gonna give Jimmy a head start down the mountain."

His companion nods his head, and their grip tightens. I feel my anger and anxiety rising. I react without thought.

"I'll have you both arrested! Johnny has committed crimes, so you have been harboring and are now assisting a criminal."

"Sounds like law talk to me."

I try to pull away, and in the process, shake one foot free and kick the one holding my feet. I stand up and begin turning my body side to side rapidly. The other boy loses his grip and falls to the ground. This happens in seconds, and before the boys can recover, I escape. I make a path through the same trees and toward the lake that Johnny used for his escape. I try to estimate how much time has passed—five minutes, maybe more. The boys aren't following.

I arrive at The Loch, but I see no sign of Johnny.

Could he be hiding somewhere near? Could he have gone higher up the mountain? Is he making his way down the mountain?

I rush up to a higher vantage point overlooking the lake and there I see a young couple sitting on the rocks. I rush over to them.

"Excuse me, did either of you see a young boy running by here a few minutes ago?"

"We did. He started down that path over there as if to go around the lake but then turned around and went over to the trail on the far side."

"Thanks so much."

I quickly run down the embankment and down a path that leads toward the back of a sign that welcomes hikers to The Loch.

I see no other way and decide he must have gone down. I follow.

In the first five minutes, I fell three times. The last is more serious than the first two. My leg is scraped and bleeding pretty badly. It appears to be a surface wound, but there is a lot of missing skin. What hurts most is my left knee, and worse, I think I sprained my right ankle. I can walk, but running or even jogging down the mountain is not going to happen. I can feel anger boiling inside.

Why didn't I sneak up on them?

It is stupid to try and run down a steep mountain on loose gravel.

Fewer rest stops are required on the way down; however, my ankle is really swelling and getting very sore, which is slowing me down. I stop to catch my breath; I check to see if my cell phone is working.

Finally, I have a signal beside a waterfall with less than a mile to go.

"Yes!"

My most conservative calculation is that Johnny has at least a thirty-minute head start. I call the Rocky Mountain National Park Headquarters and then the police station in Estes Park to tell them I have seen him. Then I call Margaret.

Chapter 12

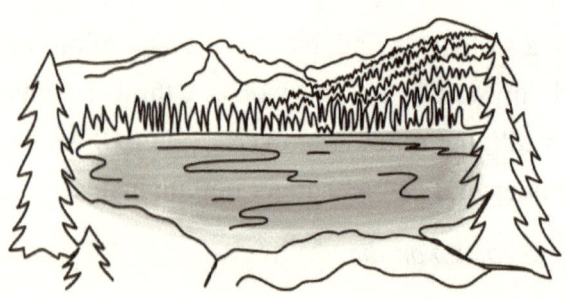

I look behind me for Dad and don't see any sign of him. I'm exhausted. I reach the edge of Bear Lake. Not wanting to draw attention to myself, I've slowed my pace. I wave and say hello to people who are either resting or making the climb. I'm sure Dad will ask every climber if they saw someone who looked like me.

I sit down in a secluded spot and decide to take a chance of being traced and make two important calls on the prepaid cell phone Fred gave me. I need to find some help as I've got no idea where to go next. I first leave a message on Fred's cell; I'm glad he doesn't answer. I tell him that I am okay, that I had met some friends and had been camping with them. I tell him thanks for everything. Next, I dialed the number Waldo gave me.

"Mr. Emerson, this is Jimmy Olson."

"Jimmy, I've been worried about you; your story is all over the news."

"Well, sir, you said to call you if I was ever in trouble, and believe me, I'm in a heap of it."

"What's your trouble; what's wrong?"

"My dad tracked me down. I saw him face-to-face just an hour ago. He snuck up on me in the mountains, demanding I come home with him. My friends held him, and I ran as fast as I could down the mountain."

"Jimmy, I'm not sure what to tell you. According to the stories I've heard and read, your dad seems like a concerned father who wants desperately to find you. He claims he and your mother love you. He admits he hasn't been a good father; he plans to turn over a new leaf."

"He's lying."

"I saw him on a television news program, and he convinced me that he was sincere."

"It's all a big cover-up. He's trying to save his reputation. He looked so anxious and angry."

"I'm impressed that he admitted he had a drinking problem and occasionally yelled at you. He said he was sorry and wants you to come home and work it out."

I can't believe what I'm hearing. I'm thinking Waldo is part of a master plan to capture me. I don't know what to believe or who to trust when he breaks the silence.

"I'm willing to contact your Dad and be the go-between between the two of you. I can speak for you to him and speak for him to you, but not reveal your whereabouts."

"But where can I hide? I'm sure the police and park rangers are trying to find me. What if they get to me first?"

"Well, we can tell him to call off all the authorities, and then you will talk. He must show you that you can trust him; that's fair."

"Okay, Waldo, I trust you. Please call him."

"In the meantime, you should be safe in public at Bear Lake; he won't want to make a scene; it would be too embarrassing."

I say goodbye, cradle my face in my hands, and wait.

#

The 60 minutes I wait feel like hours. I keep walking around the lake. I think moving keeps me safer, and I can better watch for him if I have different viewpoints along the lake shore. I stop at the hidden benches near the water so I can glance between the trees across the lake. I'm worried he could come up behind me, as that's the only direction I can't watch. I'm not sure what I will do if he catches me. I think I'll yell for help and hope someone stops to ask questions.

Waldo calls back and says that Dad agreed to talk through him, and, most importantly, promised to call off the police. He said he had an idea of where I could go, and he'd call back after checking on somewhere for me to go.

Chapter 13

Margaret answers the phone immediately and speaks before I can say a word.

"Stop chasing him!"

"How do you know what has happened?"

"I got a call from a man named Waldo, who is talking to Johnny. He gave me a perfect description of Johnny and said he got a call a few minutes ago from him. He knows Johnny is in Colorado and says Johnny trusts him. He told me Johnny was afraid. He wants us to call off the police and whoever else. Johnny said if we call the search off, he will talk to us through this man. He's going to call me back in a few minutes."

"Ok, you tell him that I'll gladly talk through him to Johnny, and I'll quit chasing him. Let's take a chance and call off the authorities. Maybe this Waldo guy will call us. It's obvious Johnny doesn't trust me. You should have seen the horror in his eyes when I confronted him on the mountain. It was awful."

"Robert, I don't know who to call; you will have to do it."

"I will. When this Waldo calls back, tell him that I'm calling everyone off and that we'll wait for further word from him."

"Why don't I have him call you? I can give him your number."

"Good idea."

"I love you, Robert."

"I love you too, Maggie; let's hope this is for real. I'll try not to mess it up like I have everything else."

I call the authorities and tell them I found Johnny and am in contact with him. I ask them not to pick him up and to call off the search. I call Margaret.

"It's done; has he called back?"

"No, not yet," replies Margaret.

"Give him my number when he does, and ask how Johnny is doing. Tell him to tell Johnny I love him and that I'm sorry I scared him. Tell him to let Johnny know I want to change my ways and want this to end. I want to get on the path to being a family again."

"I'll do that, Robert. Now, go back to the motel and find some bandages. You need to see a doctor as soon as possible."

"I will."

I head to the hotel to clean up and wait for Mr. Emerson to call.

#

My phone rings, and I jump up to answer.

"Mr. Westwood, this is Waldo Emerson. Call me Waldo."

"As you might imagine, Waldo, I've been waiting anxiously for this call."

"I certainly can understand. I have a brother in Colorado who knows everything and who is taking care of your son. I want to assure you that Johnny is safe and is in good hands."

"I'm so happy to hear that."

"My brother will talk with you face-to-face. I'm in Illinois and can't be there at any reasonable time. Is that all right?"

"In Illinois? Why Illinois? Johnny is in Colorado?"

"It's a long story, and I'll let my brother tell it to you. Are you willing to meet with him? His name is Mike."

"Yes, sure. When?"

"He has your cell number, and I'm sure he will call sometime today. I'll call him after we hang up. Robert, we aren't professionals by any stretch of the imagination. We understand you are a lawyer, and that worries us. Waldo and I agree but are quite frankly flying by the seat of my pants. We simply want to help, to get things understood and ironed out between you and your son. Right now, Johnny is afraid of you, Robert, and that is the big stumbling block to this whole thing. Mike and I understand his feelings, and we like and care about him. We're willing to play any role that might work to bring this to some sort of peaceful outcome."

"If you're not a professional, what is it that you do, Waldo?"

"I'm a truck driver, and my brother works with horses."

"I see."

"We're trying to help your son, that's all."

"Well, that's enough for me. I'll look forward to your brother's call."

Robert calls to update Margaret.

"Waldo called. His brother, Mike, will meet with me. Maggie, I'm so worried. He said Johnny was afraid of me."

"Try to figure out some way to convince him that you plan to turn your life around. He's got to believe you. If he doesn't, I think we may have lost him forever."

"I'll do my best."

I hang up and wait for more instructions from Waldo.

I have to let Waldo and Johnny control what happens, or I will lose him again.

I need a drink. Luckily, there is no alcohol in the room, and I'm not leaving until I hear more.

Chapter 14

My phone rings, and I nearly fall off the rock I'm resting on.

"Jimmy, I have spoken to my brother Mike. He is there in Estes Park as a ranch manager for the white hotel in the center of town named The Stanley."

"Yes, I saw that hotel; it's huge."

"Mike said you can stay there while we straighten things out with your dad. He is a good man and will be a big help in talking to your father. I need you to go to the Stanley and go to the barn around the back; ask for Mike. Can you get there?"

"Yes, I can take a shuttle from here. I'll watch closely to make sure Dad isn't on it."

"I spoke to your Dad, and he's in a hotel room, so you're safe to go to the *Stanley*."

"Thank you, Waldo. I'll leave now and find Mike."

"Jimmy, I'll stay in touch and be working on this behind the scenes."

#

I arrive at the stables. Many horses stand around the barn. I walk over to the fence and pat one on the head. I don't know anything about horses, but I sure would like to learn.

A tall man walks over and reaches to shake my hand.

"My name is Bill. What can I do for you?"

"I'm looking for Mike Emerson; he's expecting me."

Bill motions for me to follow him. We walk into the stable area where the horses are eating hay and what looks like oats. An older man than Bill, possibly twice his age, is on a stool bent down as he works on the hoof of one of the horses.

"Hey, Mike, this guy says you're expecting him. His name is Jimmy Olson, like in Superman."

"Didn't expect you here so soon, Jimmy. Nice to meet you," Mike says.

"Well, Jimmy, I'm going to leave you here with this old grouch," Bill says.

"Well, now, Waldo has told me about everything, Jimmy, including that I should call you Jimmy, not Johnny; is that right?"

"Yes, sir, if you don't mind. I'm grateful that you're letting me stay here."

"You can thank my boss and his buddy up at the Big House. I had to obtain permission to let you bunk with a couple of the stable hands

126

and me. Come on, I'll show you where we hang our hats and bunk down for the night."

It's a small room but with about five bunks, one on top and one on the bottom of each bed.

"You can have any one of those two over there. There are only three of us who use this room so you can choose the top or bottom of either one, it doesn't matter. We have plenty of blankets, and believe me, you will need them."

"Thank you." I walk over to the bunk with a window and put my bag up top.

"Relax, Jimmy; your story and problems are going to be safe back here. I'd like permission to tell the two other guys who helped me. They're up in the mountain with guests on four of our horses. They're good guys and won't spill the beans about why you're here; what do you say?"

"No problem; should I tell them or you?"

"I think it is best if you tell them. I'd like to hear your side of the story anyway. All I know is what Waldo has told me. I suspect there is more. In the meantime, let me introduce you to the other guys and find you some lunch. When Bill comes back, he can put you to work."

#

I meet Dave and Andrew and they invite me to sit down and have some lunch. I force myself to eat slowly so they don't guess how hungry I am. The two of them tease one another and share stories about the guests they have been helping today. I like that I'm not the center of attention now. They make me laugh, and it feels good.

"Well, Jimmy, what's the story?"

This is unexpected. I gather my thoughts.

"It's a long story."

John replies. "We got plenty of time; none of us are going anywhere."

Mike walks in and overhears the comment. He nods at me, and so I decide I must lay it all out there and be honest. I need these men to help me. I tell them my entire story.

"Fifty miles on the Mississippi River on a raft? You must've known what you were doing; that is dangerous."

"How in the world did you get all the way here?"

I continued telling them about sleeping under the overpass, meeting Waldo, and going to Denver, Breckenridge, and Vail.

All three men were listening closely. They had not seen any of the news coverage and were hearing this for the first time. In recounting the entire saga, I realized how crazy it all sounded. I've come a long way.

"Someone saw me and told the authorities. My Dad figured out that I had not drowned but that I had cut the ropes on the raft to stage the crash. When fleeing from Breckenridge by taking a shuttle to Vail, Colorado I saw my picture on the front page of the *USA Today!* "

"So, how did you make it from Vail to Estes Park?" John asks.

"I met a man named Fred, and he offered me a ride."

Since I am proud of my hike to Loch Vale, The Loch, and climbing further to Looking Glass Lake, Sky Pond, and near Andrews Glacier, I tell them in detail about building the shelter and surviving the blizzard. I have them on the edge of their chairs. They can tell that it was perhaps the most exciting and memorable moment in my life, and it was.

I proceed to describe retreating down the mountain, finding the two boys in their tent, and suddenly being face-to-face with my father.

"No wonder you ran; I would've run too, and it's good that those boys tackled him."

"No kidding. When I reached the bottom of the mountain, I remembered the cell phone that Fred bought me and called Waldo. And here I am. He told me to hitch a ride here and find his older brother Mike."

"Waldo told me he had your father call off the cops and park rangers and was volunteering to be a mediator between the two of you. Is that it?" Mike asks.

"Yes, but I'm not sure I want to communicate with my father."

"Jimmy, how did your dad know you were up on that mountain?"

"I've thought about that a lot. I guess that my mom reminded him that it was my favorite place out here."

"Well, Mike will set your father straight. He used to be quite a drinker, too, but not anymore. He's a sober man these days. Sounds to me like your Dad needs to wake up like good 'ole Mike here did."

Mike is not embarrassed. I can tell by his smile that he's proud that he stopped drinking. It must take a lot of courage. I can't imagine my dad being caught dead at an Alcoholics Anonymous meeting. I choose not to say anything.

"Well, young lad, you gotta be tired; it's late. We can talk about all this stuff later; I'm going to bed," Mike says as he rises and walks into the bunkroom.

I climb up on the top bunk and look at some bright stars out the window. I'm so tired, but I can't go to sleep. I'm scared to talk to Dad. It sounds like Waldo might do the talking. Sounds like Mike has a story to tell; I wonder if he will share it with me.

#

The stable hands are up and at it early in the morning. Mike is sweeping out the stables while Dave and John prepare the horses for their first ride of the day. Mike looks up and smiles at me.

"I'd like to step in for Waldo as your mediator with your Dad if that's okay. Waldo and I feel I should meet face-to-face with your father, and it is too difficult for Waldo to get here to do it. What do you say?"

"I still don't know how this is going to work, but sure, Mike, that will be fine.

"In the meantime, how about you helping me clean the stalls and do a little work around here? We have a program here where young people can work, and they receive room and board for free in exchange. The other young people started two days ago but you are welcome to join now if you like."

"I'd love to. I love horses and am anxious to learn. I appreciate your help."

"Now, about your Dad. I'm going to call him and meet with him face to face. I like to look a man in the eye to determine if they are being honest. My dad was an alcoholic, so I've been where you are. Let's see what his intention truly is."

"That's a perfect plan. In the meantime, tell me where to find work."

Bill shows me how to shovel the horse manure. It's now my job to make sure the horses stay clean. I'm working hard when I see Mike enter the stables and walk toward me.

"Jimmy, let's take a break. You're doing good work. I hope you like it, and shoveling manure is not the most pleasant thing to do."

"Not so bad, Mike. I appreciate the opportunity to earn my keep around here."

"I'm going to try to set up a meeting with your father sometime after lunch. If you can help the two of them with whatever makes sense, please do, Okay?"

"Sure, but tell me more about what you will say to my Dad."

"Jimmy, I think I'll first try to become acquainted and then ask him what he wants me to tell you. I think that would be a start, and I promise to share everything when I get back. I won't make any promises to him, and you can decide what you want to do. How does that sound?"

"I'm really scared."

"Me too. I've never done this kind of thing before."

"I don't want Waldo, Fred, or you to get in any trouble over this. You won't tell him where I'm at, will you?"

"Of course not. I plan to park about six blocks away and walk to the coffee house to meet him. I know this guy that runs a restaurant, and he will let me park in the back; your Dad will never see my car, only me."

"Sounds good, but I'm still scared."

"There anything you want me to tell him on this first visit?"

"No, I want to hear what he has to say."

Chapter 15

I arrive early to meet Waldo's brother Mike and figure out a way to see Johnny face-to-face. I don't want to scare him off again. I sit in the front of the coffee shop in my red shirt so Mike will know who I am. A man in a flannel shirt walks directly to my table.

"Robert?"

"Yes, I assume you're Mike?"

Mike holds out his hand, and I shake it. I motion for him to sit down. The waitress comes, and he orders coffee. It's quiet here as only two other tables have people sitting there. It's relatively private.

"We finally meet; I've got to admit right up front I've never done this kind of thing before, but I'll do the best I can."

"Well, Mike, in all my years as a lawyer, I never mediated anything either. I never in my life thought I'd be meeting like this, especially in a situation where I'd be trying to save my relationship with my son. Most importantly, is he OK?"

"He's fine, I mean it. He has plenty to eat, a place to sleep at night, and we've put him to work to keep him busy."

"What kind of work? Your brother said you worked with horses."

"Well, I used to, up in Wyoming, but not anymore. It's what I've done more than anything else. Waldo for years called me 'Cowboy.'"

"What do you do now?"

"Let's say I'm a businessman and get on with what we came here to talk about."

"I'm sorry; I guess I'm a little bit nervous and want to make sure he's in good hands."

"I can understand. I'm sure you would like to know where he is, what kind of work he is doing, who we are."

"Exactly! You are good at reading minds, Mike. So, what can you tell me?"

"Jimmy, I mean, Johnny is scared. Not of who he is with, but scared of you, Robert."

I put my face in my hands.

"I've been a lousy father, no doubt about that."

"Do you want to tell me about it?"

"Yes, maybe it will help."

For the next hour, I tell Mike everything. I admit to the drinking and violence. I admit to slapping Maggie and Johnny when I've had too much to drink. I admit that I thought my public image was important so I could run for judge. But I also say I'm ready to change.

"He changed his name, Mike." I fight back the tears.

"He seems pretty much attached to Jimmy."

"I suppose so. I can't believe the planning he did and the risks he took to run away from us. It's hard not to be proud of his success. Yet, I'm terrified of what could have happened and devastated that he felt he had to go to such lengths. That he had to escape his home. I want to tell you something important, Mike; it's the most important thing I'll share today. I'm afraid you'll have to judge if it's true; there is no way for me to prove it, at least yet."

"Tell me."

"I've stopped drinking, and when I return to Missouri, I plan to go to AA meetings. I want to do this for me, not Johnny. I realize it is the only way I can win him back. I want to be a family again. I want him to love and respect me. Mike, I love him very much. I need you to tell him I promise to make it all up to him. And, one more thing, tell him I'll never hit him again."

Mike reaches over the table and puts his hand on my arm.

"I believe you."

"Thank you; it's true, I swear it."

"I know, and I'll do my best to convey what you have told me to Johnny."

"I know I have to win back his trust. I'm hopeful you or Waldo can help show me how to do that. I don't know where to start."

"I'd suggest we let Johnny tell us how and let him lead the way. I doubt this will be something that happens overnight. Robert, you can't expect him to forget everything and start over. He's convinced you might be so angry you would kill him. He's convinced you're going to lie to me and try to fool me into turning him in."

"I see your point. This is going to take time, and I need to be patient. Ask Johnny what I need to do so he believes me. What can I do to make him comfortable coming back home to his mother and me? Tell him I'll do anything."

"In the meantime, I'd like to suggest to you, if I may. I'm a recovering alcoholic myself. I suggest you find AA meetings now. There is no reason to wait. I suggest you go every day, regardless of what Johnny says. This is stressful, and quitting won't be easy. Sitting and waiting in a hotel will not accomplish a thing. Help yourself and call the national number and find a meeting. At first, I sometimes went to two a day to quit drinking."

"I trust you, Mike. I'll do it. I'll be anxiously awaiting Johnny's response, but I need to help myself, or his response won't matter. I'm not a patient man, so this is something I'm going to have to learn."

Mike stands and we shake hands again, and I leave.

Chapter 16

Mike walks into the stable and smiles. Dave and John walk in behind him.

Finally, Dave speaks up. "OK, spill the beans; how'd it go?"

Mike motions for us to head outside to the picnic table. He gets in the cooler, grabs us all a water bottle, and sits down.

"It went much better than I thought it would."

I breathe a sigh of relief at those words. I take a deep breath and prepare myself to hear the rest. At least he didn't say Dad was angry and wanted to kill me or that he threatened Mike if he didn't send me back.

"It's important for you to know, Jimmy, that I'm not taking sides. I want what is best for you, and I want to try to be as impartial as I can."

"I trust you, Mike, and I promise to listen."

"Jimmy, he admitted to everything. He admitted to drinking and even to being violent. He understands your fear. He wants you to know he has already quit drinking and that he is willing to do whatever it takes to make you comfortable to come home."

"Wait, he admitted to hitting us?"

"Yes. He admits to being a bad father in every way."

"You believe him? Besides the tears, what convinced you?"

"He said there was no way he could prove that he was going to stop drinking. That only he could do it, and he had to do it for him, not for you. I think he was trying to say he had to respect himself before he could expect you to do it. And he claims the most important thing in the world for him is to win over your love and respect. It takes a long time to develop trust, and I think he knows it doesn't happen overnight."

"I didn't see that one coming. I thought he would demand to know where I was and threaten to have you arrested if you did not tell him. So what do we do now?" Jimmy asks.

"Well, he agreed to let you decide what happens next. I told him I'd call tomorrow to set up a time and place to share with him your response to what he has said."

Andrew says, "Jimmy, think about it for a while; don't make any rash decisions. We're here for you to bounce ideas off us. If you need more time, Mike can tell your Dad that you need more time. There is no rush to this."

"John's right," chimed in Dave, "You don't have to be alone on this; you got friends here."

"Let's talk after dinner, then take a long walk and think it over. The mountains can be very calming and soothing. I often look there for answers," Mike says.

"OK, I don't feel like eating; maybe I'll head that way for a while."

I'm so confused. I didn't expect this at all. I want so badly to believe him. I want to believe he loves me and that he will not drink and hit me ever again. I want to see Mom smile, and I want to have a life like my friends. But it is just too good to be true. People don't change that fast. I can't take a chance. I think he could be putting on a show, and as soon as I come home, he could lock me in my room for life. I've heard him tell Mom he would quit drinking before, and it lasted one day at the most."

I hear someone approaching from behind me. I glance over my shoulder; it is Dave.

"Do you want company on your walk?"

I need someone to help me think about this. We walk away from camp.

We walk for about a half-mile without saying anything. The tips of the mountains reflect the setting sun; soon, they will be in the shadow of the range to the West. It's a beautiful evening, and before long, the stars will take over the sky.

"What would you do?"

"Like I said, I'd trust Mike. If Mike believes him, then I'd try. He needs to prove what he is promising. How much time? And how do you prove something like that? I don't know. Jimmy, my father, was also an alcoholic; it's a vicious thing. In AA, they call it a cunning and baffling disease, and devastating too."

We head back to the bunkhouse, and I find Mike.

"Do you think he will go to AA?"

"I don't know, Jimmy, and there is no guarantee that it will work. It is up to your Dad, no one else. I've been sober for slightly more than two years. I go to AA meetings at least three times a week. I feel good after every meeting, and, ironically, I am getting well by listening to a lot of sick people. They understand me; they have been where I have been, and they don't judge me. The only goal is to stay sober and not take another drink. I have to tell you that many don't make it; some come back, but many don't. I've got no idea how many succeed; I would guess about half."

"Not very positive odds."

"Fifty-fifty, when you consider that if they keep drinking, they will most likely ruin their lives forever and may die from it. Look at your dad. He has lost his son! You're scared of him, and now he cries out of remorse that he has made a mistake."

"What happened to your dad?"

"I don't know; I guess that he is dead. Maybe there could be a waiting period, a time for your dad to prove that he is serious."

"How long?"

"I don't know, enough time to make you feel comfortable. Maybe you could have a weekly phone call at first, with your mom too. And if things begin to look better, you could then see him. You need to decide what will make you believe him and trust him again."

I don't know what to think. I would love to stay with Mike and with Dave and John too. Is Mike serious? Does he mean I can stay with them at the stables? Do you mean I can stay here and work while Dad proves himself to me?"

"I'm sure. We need the help, and with your Dad's permission and the proper paperwork, we can formally make you a part of our internship while you wait."

"I'd love to work with you guys, even if it was just for the summer."

"Does this mean you think the idea of proposing some kind of 'test period' for your father is worth considering?"

"Yes, I love it."

"Do you think if your father agrees to it, that you would be willing to meet with him before he heads back to Missouri? I think he needs to hear it first hand from you, see that you are OK living with us, and be assured about weekly or agreed-upon calls. What do you say?"

"I understand, but I'll have to think about that last one."

I walk into the stables to see Flash, my favorite horse. Everyone leaves me alone.

Stroking the side of Flash's head, the horse looks at me as if he's willing to listen.

I climb up on the edge of a stable railing.

"OK, Flash, here's the deal. What if I could trust Dad again? What if I could go home someday? That would be so awesome. I miss Mom." Flas nods and stares at me.

"I want to believe him; on the other hand, if it is a trick, a lie, then what do I do?" Flash stares at me without taking his eyes away.

"OK, I'll agree to meet with him. I'm pretty sure I can know if he's lying if I can look at his face. I can see that mean, angry man behind a smile. I've seen it for years."

I run back to Mike and the guys at the table.

"Let's do it."

"That-a-way to go, Jimmy, it's the right thing to do. I'll set it up. You decide what it is you would want your Dad to do to prove to you he is serious."

Chapter 17

I look at my leather engraved calendar, Robert B. Westwood III. Things like this are no longer important to me. How crazy I was to think it mattered. I try to work in my hotel room to pass the time as I wait for a call from Mike. I'm waiting to call Margaret until I know more. I don't want to get her hopes up if this doesn't work.

The waiting is agonizing, and I'm surprised how much I want a drink. This would be a lot easier if I had a drink to calm me down. I think about Mike's suggestion to find an AA meeting in Estes. He's got a point that this stress doesn't help matters and perhaps getting started here would be easier than back home. Then the phone rings.

"Robert, he will meet with you."

"I can never repay you for making this happen."

"How about tomorrow morning at the same coffee shop, around 10 a.m.?"

"Sounds reasonable."

"Mr. Westwood, I think it's important for you to understand that Jimmy is nervous about this conversation, and regardless of the outcome, he won't be going back to Missouri with you."

"I understand."

"And one more thing, and I'm sorry to have to say this, but you're a lawyer and have lots of connections. If I see any sign of police or investigators or other people who may try something stupid, you may never see me or your son again."

"Believe me, Mike, I appreciate everything you're doing. There is no way I want to jeopardize this chance in any way to earn my son's respect and love. It'll only be me at the coffee shop. I promise. I don't want to blow this chance."

"OK then, see you at 10 a.m."

I call Maggie and tell her the whole story and all about the arranged meeting in the morning.

"I'm going to find an AA meeting this evening. I want a drink so bad."

"That's a great idea."

I call and got the national AA number, and they refer me to two local groups. One has a meeting a block from my hotel in an hour. I'm committed to going; I've got to make it through tonight.

The hour passes by at a snail's pace. I take a deep breath and walk down the street to a small church where it is supposed to be. I nod at a couple of guys standing outside smoking, and I open the door and walk into a big hall with several people standing around and chatting.

"Are you here for the meeting?"

"Yes, am I in the right place?"

"Grab a cup of coffee and sit down; we are going to start in a couple of minutes. Welcome, we are glad you are here."

Chapter 18

Mike walks into the stable as I'm cleaning the stalls. I stop and look up at him to learn more.

"Did you talk with my dad? Do we have a meeting?"

"If you are ready to meet with your father face-to-face, it is all set for tomorrow at 10 a.m."

"Ok, let's see if he's for real."

I jump into Mike's truck.

"Jimmy, we are going to drive around a little bit; your dad promised no shenanigans, but I want to make sure he is the only one around. After all, you were national news for a long time. I don't want any unexpected company."

"You mean police?"

"Yeah, or anyone else, even a friend of your father."

"Mike, I'm so glad you thought of that."

We drive around and see nothing unusual and park in the back lot of Mike's restaurant friend.

"You stay here. I'm going to check out the riverwalk area and the outside coffee shop patio; I'll be back in about 15 minutes. Is that OK with you?"

"Sure, no problem."

The minutes seem like hours. Mike returns as promised and we begin walking toward the river.

"Is he there?"

"Yes, I saw him; I don't think he saw me. Now, Jimmy, I want you to know we can leave the conversation at any time; let me know when you're ready to go."

"Will you speak first?"

"Sure; try to be polite. I sense that he is serious and won't insist on anything or do anything that will turn you away. At least, I hope so."

I see him sitting at the table through the window. My heart beats so hard I think it will pop through my chest. I walk behind Mike, trying to hide.

As we approach, Dad jumps up from his chair to greet us. He reaches out like he wants to hug me, but Mike steps in and holds out his hand to shake Dad's.

"Hi, Johnny, it's so good to see you."

"Thanks."

We sit down opposite Dad, and for about 10 seconds, no one says anything.

"Well, here we are. Maybe a way to start would be for you, Robert, to share with us how you found Johnny."

"Sure."

Dad starts from the beginning. He calmly goes through the timeline and tells the story. I wait for him to yell at me or say something about how much trouble I have caused them. He says none of that. And then, as he finishes, I see tears in his eyes. Real tears; he isn't faking it.

"Johnny, I love you so much. I am so sorry; your mother and I have been worried sick. Are you OK?"

Mike looks and says, "It's your turn."

"I'm sorry I caused you so much grief, but I'm fine. I have a job, nice friends that I work with, plenty of food, and a shelter over my head. You and Mom don't need to worry about me; I've grown up quite a bit in the last couple of months."

More silence. Dad looks at Mike.

"Mr. Westwood, Jimmy, I mean Johnny, and I've had some long talks about what he would like to do. As he says, he is safe with us, and we are surrounded by a safe environment. My fellow workers and I have offered him a job for the summer. I would rather not tell you where that is right now, but perhaps sometime in the future. Johnny proposes a trial period via telephone calls to bring you up to date about his activities, and you can share what is happening back in Missouri. How does that sound?"

Before Dad can answer, I have to know.

"Have you stopped drinking, Dad?"

"Johnny, I have not had a drink since reading your letter. I went to an AA meeting last night, and I plan to go every day, no matter where I am, until I'm no longer craving a drink. I know it will be tough, and I'll be doing it for me as much as for you. I'm ready to change my life and ways, and I've you to thank for that."

I think he means it.

He reaches over to touch my hand.

"Not yet, Dad. Let's see how this plan works out, OK?"

"Ok, son."

Dad does not look embarrassed or angry that I don't want him to touch me. He doesn't lose his temper or demand anything. I don't know who this person is; he's so different from the Dad I left.

"So Robert, who makes the first call, and how frequently?"

"I guess once a day is too often, but will a weekly chat work?"

"Let's set a date and time, and I'll call from here. I need a phone."

"I'll find you a cell phone, no problem, Johnny. I'll leave it at the desk at the hotel with your name on it. Use it anytime for anything. How about every Sunday evening at about 7 p.m.? Your Mom and I will be anxiously waiting."

"OK, let's try it and see how it works out."

"I've got a favor to ask, Johnny. Would you please say hi to your mother if I call her right now? She is so anxious to hear your voice. I know I'm to blame, so please give her some comfort."

He holds up his cell phone, waiting for me to answer.

"I'd love to talk to Mom. Please go ahead and call her."

He dials immediately.

"Maggie, Johnny is here and wants to say hi."

He hands me the phone.

"Hi, Mom. I miss you. I'm fine, so please don't worry. Are you OK? Has Dad been mean to you or taking any of this out on you?"

"Johnny, your Dad has done nothing but blame himself. Please come home; we can work this out."

"I will stay here and let Dad work on his drinking this summer. I'll call you every Sunday to check-in. I can't come home until I know I'm safe, Mom."

"Ok, Johnny, you do what you need to do. Please stay safe. I'll look forward to every single call."

"I gotta go, Mom. I love you. Bye."

"One more thing. Dad, will you promise to inform the authorities that all is OK and to call off the search?"

"I already did, Johnny, but don't be surprised if someone recognizes you and causes you trouble. If this happens, have them call me; that goes for you too, Mike, OK?"

"OK, sounds good to me."

"Johnny, I'm going back to Missouri in the morning. If you need anything or want to talk, please call me. Do you have my cell phone number?"

"OK, Dad, I will. Please find me a cell phone, and I'll pick it up tomorrow."

"Do you need any money or anything else?"

"I'm fine. I'm working and doing ok."

"Alright, I'll talk with you on Sunday. Thanks, Mike, for all your help."

We shake hands, and Mike and I leave first. We take an indirect route back to the truck to make sure we aren't followed. Near the truck, we go into a store to make sure. We wait half an hour before getting into the truck and heading to the stables.

#

"Well, that went pretty well, don't you think?"

"Yes, I think so."

"Are you OK with these telephone calls?"

"Thanks. Are you sure you want to give me a job and keep me around?"

"Absolutely!"

"Do you think he'll stop drinking?"

"No guarantee, kiddo, I hope so. I've learned in AA that you take it a day at a time; some can do it, and some can't. If you want, I'll take you to what we call an 'open meeting.' You can see for yourself how it works."

"I would like that very much."

When we returned to the stables, Dave and John wanted to hear all the details.

"OK, Jimmy, we are going to have you clean the stables, and that means more than manure. After cleaning, you can feed the horses and after that, clean the harnesses, bits, and most of all, make sure the saddles are in good shape and also clean. How does that sound?"

"I love the horses. I think they are getting to know me, too."

"Excellent. John is the expert on saddles and other equipment. I'll let him teach you the ropes, and at any time, be sure to ask any of us about anything you don't understand. We'll be here to help you; remember, all of us had to start this way, too."

"Would one of you teach me how to ride?"

"Well, since I'm the best rider, it should be me!" Dave said with a smile.

"When can we start?"

"Right now, if you'd like. Let's start easy. King Joe is an old guy and a pro; he knows the various trails we take, and if he gets loose, he will always make his way back to the stables. After several lessons and a few practice rides, if your chores are done, we will treat you as if you're a guest who has declared they are a 'beginner,' and you can tag along when we go out for rides. How does that sound?"

"Wow, that sounds awesome!"

It's mid-afternoon when Dave has a chance to teach some of the fundamentals. He starts showing me how to saddle and prepare the horse for riding, and then, using King Joe, he has me sit on the fence rail while he demonstrates how to turn him, lead him, stop him, and more. Letting the horse know that the rider was the boss, firm but kind in the process, and never yelling or screaming commands was important learning.

Dave switches places with me, and once I am aboard King Joe, he has me not only do what I was taught but also say out loud what I am doing and why I am doing it.

"OK, Jimmy, tomorrow afternoon, if you've finished cleaning and feeding the horses, I'll take you on our trail for beginners. If we have guests along, I want you to do whatever I tell them to do. As you develop more skills, we'll increase the level of difficulty, and I promise you, by the end of the month, I'll have you with me to the top of Mummy Range. That's our advanced ride, and I think by then, you'll be up for it. Sound good?"

"That sounds great! King Joe, I expect you to be my teacher, too."

The next afternoon, Mike goes to the hotel to get my cell phone. Dad also gives him $100 and asks him to help me get a bank account so they can send me money if I need it. Mike and I go to the bank in the afternoon to set things up. A nice young lady named Gail helps us. I now have a bank account.

On the way out of the bank, I notice a picture of me on a bulletin board, asking for leads to my whereabouts and offering a $1,000 reward and a note to call Robert Westwood.

"Mike, look at this. If anyone sees this I could be in trouble. I thought Dad stopped the search!"

"I'm sure he did; this is just left over. Here, let's take it down."

How long will it take for word to spread? I'm no longer missing, and there is no longer a reward.

On Sunday, I call home and talk for 15 minutes. I ask Dad again if he has halted the search and tell him about the poster. He assures me it's all called off, and that must have been a leftover. Mom and Dad let me talk about what I want and they listen. Then they each talk to me and tell me about their week. Dad talks a lot about what AA meetings are like and says he's making friends. He also says he decided not to run for judge but to focus on our family, so he withdrew from the election. I never thought he would give that up for me.

Mike takes me to an AA meeting so I can see what they are like. The people sit in a circle and each takes a turn. Mike told me before we came what I should say.

"My name is Jimmy, and my father is an alcoholic. I'm here to learn and understand my father."

"Welcome, Jimmy. We are glad you are here and hope that hearing our story can help you. My name is Ted, and I am an alcoholic. I drank too much for years and lost my wife and my ten-year-old daughter because of it. I haven't seen my daughter since. I don't know where they are, so I've not been able to make amends. After they left, I drank even more. I walked in these doors five years ago and have been sober since. Every day is a battle. I would love nothing more than to take a drink, but I know that one drink would take me right back to the misery I had when I quit. I had to hit bottom, to admit I was helpless, and alcohol was the reason. This group taught me that and showed me the 12 steps to getting better. Today, I'm a grateful alcoholic."

"My name is Alex, and I'm an alcoholic. I'll pass, as I'm here to listen."

"My name is Sharon, and I'm an alcoholic. My father and mother were alcoholics. Liquor was the solution to all my problems until it became the problem. I've been arrested for DWI three times and lost my license, my job, and my children. I'm working hard to make amends. I come here three times a week, sometimes four. I'm not alone here, and no one is afraid to tell me exactly how things are. They set me straight and seem to know when I'm seriously working the program and when I'm trying to shortcut."

The people are so honest. I walk away knowing this is a long process and very hard. I also see that people have lost their families, and their children have suffered like me. The meetings are like Dad described; I'm convinced he is going to them.

#

I can't believe it's been a month since I started riding and since Dad left me at Estes Park with Mike and the guys. Time has gone by quickly.

Every Sunday, I talk with Mom and Dad. Dad continues to go to AA meetings, and Mom says he's acting like the man she married. I love working at the stables, and Mike says my skills are improving every day. I've been able to get chores done early in the day so I can go on the rides with the guests. I've been on almost all the trails. I've graduated from riding lessons, so I can now ride Flash. He's a strong but reliable horse that had considerable experience on the more difficult trails. He is named Flash because when he was young, lightning struck within a few feet of him. He was so shocked that he broke through a weak spot in the fence and was gone "in a flash."

Flash and I are becoming friends. We trust each other to do the right thing when faced with decisions about which path to take, how to avoid loose rocks and hanging branches, and when to speed up and when to slow down. I decide to take him for a short ride down by the stream behind the stables.

I stop to enjoy the sounds of the stream when I notice two people across the stream talking. I can just make out what they are saying. I noticed the one lady was from the bank; she had helped me open my checking account.

"Gail, I have this buddy of mine that I think came to Estes to find a summer job. His name is Johnny Westwood."

What? He's no friend of mine. Why is he talking about me?

I listen more carefully, petting Flash to keep him quiet.

The young couple are having a picnic in the woods, and I pause to listen.

"Jordan, why do you mention your friend?"

"Well, I was wondering if a young man with that name had come into the bank to open an account. I've been looking all over town for him and can't find him."

"I can't see any harm in telling you that a young man named Westwood did open an account recently. He was a nice kid. Do you want me to tell him about you the next time he comes in?"

"Oh no, Gail, I would much rather it be a surprise. If this guy listed Cape Girardeau as his hometown, he's my friend. If you could check that out and give me his address in Estes, then I could show up and surprise the hell out of him. I'm sure he would love it."

"Ok, I will look it up tomorrow."

"Thank you, Gail. That would be perfect."

What is going on with this stranger looking for me and wanting my address? Could he be one of those people they warned me about who would be looking for me for a reward? What if Dad hired him to find me and bring me home? Maybe he hasn't changed at all.

I head back to the stables to think about this some more and perhaps obtain some advice. When I arrive, the guys are out on a trail ride with some customers and Mike has gone into town. I look over at the road leading into the stables and see the guy by the stream driving up to the stables. I panic. This guy, for whatever reason, is after me. I have to leave now!

I run into the bunkhouse, grab a bunch of my things, and jump on Flash to ride out of there and hide. We take off at full speed toward the mountains which I have come to know so well. The sun is setting as I reach the peak behind the Stanley. This is not a long-term solution but at least I'm safe for now.

"Looks like we will be spending the night here, Flash. I'm sorry about supper, but we could not risk going into town. My dad has let me down again and has sent this Jordan after me. I'm sure of it. Dad was trying to convince me to come home last Sunday."

I decide I better build a shelter of some kind and prepare for nightfall. I tie Flash to a tree and remove his saddle so he can rest. I grab a couple of shirts and arrange them so that at least they will keep the dew of the night off me as I sit up to sleep. My heart is still racing as I try to relax.

My only hope is that the guys will protect me and realize what I have done when I don't show up. They will know I don't have any long-lost friends looking for me in Estes Park. They will notice Flash is missing as well and can figure out where I've gone and come to help me tomorrow. I know I can count on them.

The sounds of the night are pretty scary up here. At Sky Pond, it was quiet, but here I'm in the woods, and there are many animals around. I hear owls, wind in the trees, a coyote howling, and other mysterious night sounds. Suddenly, I hear the trees and the brush nearby rustling.

What is that? Could it be a bear? What am I going to do? I'm here in the open, lying on the ground; it's just me and Flash.

Flash begins to stir and snort and even kick his hoof on the ground. I need to check on Flash and make sure he is secure and safe. I open my eyes and peek around the shirt draped over me. It's a bear! A black bear makes it hard to see even in the full moon. He's about 5 feet away.

What did the guys tell me to do if I saw a bear?

I remember and begin to yell at it and bang the tree, anything to make noise. It works as he turns and runs down the mountain. That was too close! Should I still stay the night or try to make it back since everyone is there and that guy Jordan is gone? The guys can help me now that they are home. I decided Flash could help me down the mountain. I need to try to get to the stables; it is not safe here.

I saddle Flash in the dark. Flash picks his way through the trees to take us back down the mountain. I'm keeping an eye out for low-hanging branches as Flash takes one step at a time. Suddenly, Flash rears up, and I fall off, tumbling over the edge of the trail. I feel a sharp pain and come to a sudden stop as I hit something hard. The world goes completely dark.

Chapter 19

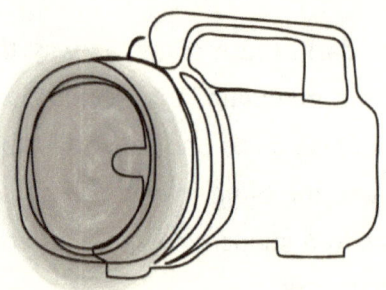

"Mr. Westwood, Robert, this is Mike from Estes Park. Sorry to awaken you at this hour."

"Mike, what's wrong? Is Johnny okay?"

"You need to get here as soon as possible. We've taken him to the hospital and are waiting for word. I know this is a shock. Call me when you are on the road to the airport, and I'll fill you in, but for now, get here ASAP."

I wake up Margaret and tell her what little I know. I have so many questions but no time. We don't even stop to pack a bag. When we load into the car, I tell Maggie to call the airport and find the first flight to Denver. We can arrive there by late afternoon if we are lucky. We book the first flight and Maggie hands the phone back.

I dial Mike's number and put him on speakerphone so Maggie can listen also.

"Mike, tell me everything. We have at least an hour and a half drive to St. Louis, even going 85mph. What has happened?"

Mike begins to tell me how Johnny was missing last night and so was his horse. They figured he was hiding because someone at the stables said a person named Jordan came in asking about him. It was dark, so they could not go looking for him. Then Johnny's horse came back without him, and they knew he was in trouble. They saddled up and went searching for him even though it was dark. The horse led them up the mountain right to a cliff. When they used the big flashlight they spotted some of his clothes in a tree first. He had rolled down a cliff, and they still could not see him. They used ropes to lower themselves down the cliff to solid ground. They found him a few feet from the cliff; he had hit his head and was unconscious.

Mike explains the challenges they had getting him out of the ravine and to the hospital. They took him to the emergency room and still don't have any information. He was alive but hadn't regained consciousness.

"Robert, I'm sorry I don't have more information. We have many more questions than we have answers. Can you call the hospital and give consent for me to manage his care until you are here? We will keep you informed the entire time, but we can't reach you except via email while you are flying."

"Of course, Mike. I'll call right away. Please have the doctor call me as soon as they come out with information."

I look at Maggie, and she is staring into space; her face has no

161

emotion. Neither of us can speak. What if he doesn't make it? He survived the river, and now this?

#

As we sit in the airport at the gate, the phone rings. Again, I put it on speaker so we can both hear.

"We have news. The doctor is here, and I asked him to wait until you were online."

"Mr. Westwood, is that you? Are you Johnny's father?"

"Yes, and his mother is here as well. We are waiting to board a plane in St. Louis and arrive as quickly as we can."

"I'm sorry to report that Johnny has a fractured skull, a serious concussion, and is not yet conscious. We are draining fluid from his brain, reducing inflammation. The good news is that we expect, with lots of rest, he will recover fully."

"When will he regain consciousness?" Margaret speaks first.

"When the anesthesia wears off, which should be in about an hour, you will be able to talk with him. I would prefer only two people at a time."

"Any other injuries?" Mike asks.

"Yes, I was coming to that. He has a broken leg that should heal nicely, a severely bruised shoulder, and many scratches and abrasions. These two, in time, will heal without serious aftereffects."

"So how long will this healing process take, doctor? When might my son be able to leave the hospital?"

"He'll be with us not less than a week, and how much more time will be determined by how well his injuries are responding to treatment. Mr. and Mrs. Westwood, I'll call with any updates. Please ask the nurse to call me when you arrive at the hospital."

"Yes, and if we are not available, please talk with Mike Emerson; we trust him totally in our absence."

"Robert, we have a room for you at the Stanley. Come straight to the hospital. When they move him to a room, I'll text you the number."

We arrive, and Johnny is still in the recovery room. He is finally transferred to a regular room. Margaret decides to spend the night with him in the hospital. I head back to the hotel to get some sleep as we figure we will be taking turns for a few days.

I wonder what happened to cause Johnny to go into the mountains alone.

Chapter 20

I open my eyes and see Mom sitting by my bedside.

"Mom? What are you doing here? Where am I? Ouch, what has happened?"

"Oh, thank God! You're in the hospital, Johnny, in Estes Park. Do you remember how you got here? You gave us quite a scare."

"I remember falling off Flash. I was riding, and now I'm here."

Mike and the guys walk in.

Mike exclaims, "Welcome back to the living, Johnny! You took ten years off our lives, and that's a lot when you are as old as we are."

They each come to the bedside and hug me.

"OK, tell me what in the world happened, Mike. How did I get here?"

"We have some of the same questions for you. When Flash showed up after dark without you, we were worried and went looking for you. He led us to where you must have fallen off, and we had to repel down a cliff to find you bleeding and unconscious. It was quite an effort to move you out of there. Naturally, we called your parents, and they came right away. That was three days ago."

"Three days? I've completely lost three days? And what did they do to me? I hurt everywhere?"

Mike pushes the button on the bed to call the nurse.

"You had a long surgery, and it's taken forever for you to wake up."

A nurse walks in with a big smile.

"So this is the Johnny everyone is talking about. Johnny, I'm so glad to finally meet you and see that smile."

"My head is hurting."

"I'll get you something straight away. In the meantime, your friends need to take it easy with you and take turns. We're all relieved, but you can't overdo it."

Sam replies, "Right away, sorry we didn't know he was awake. We'll leave, and you can visit with your mom, Jimmy."

"Thanks, Sam, but it's Johnny again. I think I'm ready to have my name back."

Everyone smiles and leaves the room. Mom has tears running down her face. She reaches over and hugs me before moving close to the bed and holding my hand.

"Johnny, is it OK if I call Dad? We've been taking turns staying with you, and he'll want to know you're OK."

"Can we talk first, Mom? Why did you let him hurt us? Why didn't you stand up to him? I understand you couldn't do it when he was angry and drunk, but why not the next morning? I don't understand why you didn't take me and leave or kick him out."

"Johnny, marriage is a complicated thing. I love your father, and I blamed myself for everything. I have been going to Al-Anon, which is a part of AA for families. I'm learning about why I responded as I did. I'm so sorry I let you down, and I did not protect you. Dad is trying hard and being successful; I'm trying too. We love you more than anything and want to be a family."

"Thank you, Mom. Is there something for kids too with AA?"

"Yes, there is, and I think it would be great if you went. Can I call your Dad now?"

"Yes, but please don't leave me when he comes; I don't want to be alone with him. I know he is trying, and our calls have gone well, but I still don't trust that he won't yell at me. I think he hired someone to find me. That's why I ran away up the mountain."

"Johnny, he didn't hire anyone. I'm sure of it. He called off all the authorities and at no point did he hire anyone. There was a reward, but we withdrew that once he saw you on the mountain. We are honoring your wishes; he doesn't want to jeopardize anything."

"We'll see; I need to ask him. I can tell when he lies. I'm going to close my eyes now. I'm tired."

She steps out of the room to call Dad. I close my eyes and think of what I'm going to say to Dad. Could she be right and that guy was operating because he had seen the reward and didn't know it was called off? I guess that makes sense. But what if Dad did secretly hire him and not tell Mom? The Dad I knew would've done it without thinking twice.

I doze off and when I awake, Mike is sitting next to me. He smiles.

"I spoke with your mom, and she thought I should talk to you and be here when you see your Dad. She mentioned you thought he hired someone to find you, and that's why you were hiding in the mountains. I thought I should tell you what we now know before you see your dad."

"Please do. Mike, I still don't trust him. I had heard Jordan talking to Gail from the bank, saying he was my friend. She must have given him the address of the stables because the next thing I knew, I saw him coming down the driveway. I grabbed Flash and headed up the mountain to hide. I'm still not ready to go home, especially if Dad is trying to trick me."

"There is no evidence that your Dad is involved other than initially offering the reward. The police talked to Jordan, who is a college student, and had seen the news about you and saw a poster with information about the reward at Bear Lake. He wanted the reward money. He hadn't heard that you had been found because we didn't contact the press. We haven't yet gotten all the posters down."

"I guess that makes sense. Thanks for telling me, Mike. I should've trusted and waited for you or the guys instead of panicking and thinking the worst."

"No one blames you, Jimmy, I mean, Johnny. We all understand and are sorry that we were all gone at the same time, and you were so afraid."

Just then, Dave walks in and pulls up a chair. There sure are a lot of people who care about me.

Mike says, "Johnny, the summer is almost over, and I think your Dad and Mom will want you to come home with them."

"They what? How do…."

Dave responds before I ask my question. "Whoa, kid. We are only guessing. If you were our son, it is exactly what we would want and you shouldn't be surprised if your Dad suggests it. Honestly, he hasn't said anything to us."

"So you guys don't want me to come back to the stables?"

"Come on, Johnny, you know that's not the case. We would love to have you back, but there are only two weeks left, and you're recovering. We're being practical. It's time to think of what comes next. You must admit the ranch is a problem with that broken leg."

They remain quiet to let the reality of the situation sink in.

"Was it my mom who asked you to say it? I know you are right, but I hadn't thought past this summer."

"No, Johnny, but think about it. You are lucky to be alive; you have a leg that's going to be in a cast for at least six weeks. The doctors have said that riding a horse for at least six months is out of the question; your skull is still cracked, and you look like you've been in a fight for the ages."

"I guess you're right, but I'll miss you guys so much."

"We'll miss you, too. We don't have to decide the next plan today, but I wanted to be honest that it's time you decide if you are ready to go home to recover or what other plan we might hatch."

Dave says, "Johnny, just a little piece of advice. If you want to make your parents the happiest parents in the whole wide world, you could ask them if you could come home with them. Be the first to mention it."

Johnny smiles. "What would I do without you guys? That's a great idea; I know they love me and after what my Dad has done about his drinking, it is time I showed a little bit of appreciation on my end. But I'm still afraid to be in the same room alone with him. My stomach hurts thinking about going back."

"Your Dad is outside waiting to see you. I'm happy to be here with you. Are you ready?"

"No, I'm not. I'm tired. Can you tell him I need to rest and think? I'll see him and Mom tonight. Mike, can you come back tonight and be here with me?"

"Sure. I think that is smart, Johnny. You woke up a few hours ago. You should be rested when dealing with your Dad."

I close my eyes, trying to imagine what going home would be like. How can I ever be in that house again? I know he says he's changed, and I know Mom says so, but I can't believe it. If I go home and he drinks and tries to hurt Mom or me, I don't think I can stand it."

#

I finish eating dinner and feel pretty good. I hear a knock at the door, and Mike walks in.

"You seem better than you did when I left. I hope you got some sleep?"

"I did. I'm ready to see them, but I still don't have a plan. I'm not ready to go home. I don't know what to do. But like you said, we have a week to decide."

Mom walks in and says, "Is it OK if we come in?"

I nod yes. I see Dad walking behind her. He has tears in his eyes.

"Johnny, I'm so glad to see you awake. I was so worried. Do you mind if I hug you?"

He steps near me, and I automatically withdraw and want to hide under the sheets. But instead of coming anyway, he steps back.

"Never mind. I see that it's still too soon. I love you, and I was scared to death we would lose you again."

Just then, Mom's cell phone rings. She looks at it and answers.

"Hello, George. Let me ask him."

She turns to me and asks, "George Olson is on the phone and wants to talk to you. Do you want to talk to him?"

"Oh yes!"

She hands me the phone.

"Mr. Olson, I'm so glad to talk to you. I'm so sorry for getting you involved in all this. I remembered everything you taught me, and it saved me several times. I miss you and Mrs. Olson."

"Mrs. Olson is on the phone as well. We miss you, Johnny, and have been so worried about you all summer. I'm so glad you are OK."

"Mr. Olson and I have been seeing your Mom and Dad every day, talking to them and supporting them. We have tried hard to be good friends since you were gone. Johnny, we want to help however we can. We care about all of you."

"Thank you, Mrs. Olson. I didn't mean to worry anyone, but I had to be safe."

"Johnny, we know this, and your Dad has been honest with us about his problems. We're here to help you. If we had known, we would have helped you before. Please know you can trust us. We're here for you."

"We don't want to keep you. You visit with your parents now, and we will talk later. Please give us a call anytime and remember we're here for you. We're happy to listen and help you sort through everything. Don't forget there is a solution for every problem, Johnny."

I hang up and look at Mom and Dad. I then stare at Mike. All three stare at me as though they can't believe I'm awake.

"Thanks for waiting to come, Dad. I'm trying to believe you. I am. I admit I thought the worst when that guy came looking for me. It's still hard to trust you."

"I know. I'm working as hard as I can to be worthy of your love. What you don't know is that my Dad was also an alcoholic. He also took his anger out on me. I wanted to run away so many times, but I never

171

dared to do it. That was my first thought when you went missing. You're stronger than I was. I was reminded of my desperation, so I know what you were feeling. I'm so sorry. Unlike my dad, I'm changing. I'm not going to die this way. I want to fight for our family. You've given me the courage to do this, even though I didn't dare to escape when I was your age."

"Wow. I had no idea. Thank you for sharing that. I don't know where I can go to recover. Honestly, I'm not ready to go home yet. I know I'll need help, and I know I can't work at the ranch. I'm sorry, I still can't go home."

"We'll all work on it, and I'm sure we can think of something. School starts in three weeks, and you must be in school. Let's think of what we can do that makes that possible. We have a few days. We can figure this out."

I'm getting tired again, so everyone leaves. I lay my head down and tried to think of a plan but quickly fell asleep.

#

I wake up refreshed and feeling so much better today. I eat my breakfast, and the doctor comes in. He says I need to start learning to walk with this cast but need to be careful, as falling could result in further injury to my head. The nurse has been helping me to the bathroom, but that's as far as I've walked. They now want me to learn to use crutches and walk up and down the halls. The doctor thinks I can go home in three days instead of a week. He asks me what my home is like. I tell him I'm not sure where I'm going home, so I don't know if it has stairs and such. I need to figure this out!

172

I remember I had a cell phone, at least if I didn't lose it when I fell. I think it was tied to Flash, so it should be OK. I call the nurse and ask her to gather my things and I find it. I wrote down Mr. Olson's number yesterday, so I'm going to call them.

"My doctor said I should be able to leave in three days. That's why I'm calling. I have to figure out a plan and thought you might be able to help me think of something. I know Dad is trying hard, and Mom too, but I'm still afraid to go home. I can't work with this broken leg, so I can't stay here, and besides, I want to start school. I'm sorry, but I can't live with Mom and Dad yet."

"Johnny, why don't you come and stay with us? We would love to have you in Jennifer's old room. You can stay here for a few weeks and heal that leg. You can visit your folks in your home to become used to it again and continue to build trust. You can attend Al-Anon meetings with your mother to learn how to best live with your father. You can also watch your father and make sure he is doing what he says he is doing. We would love to have you for as long as you need."

"Johnny, this is Mrs. Olson. I got on the phone. Come to our house and let me spoil you. I'll bake your favorite pie and help you learn to move around. We'll take you to school until that cast comes off. Jennifer's old room sits there empty. Let us help your family."

"You'd do this for me? You'd let me live with you?"

"You can stay until you feel comfortable going home. We can transition you there slowly. We'd love to help you this way. Please let us."

"You have a deal. I'll talk to Mom and Dad this morning. It's another test of Dad's willingness to let me learn to trust him. The Dad I know would never agree and would be worried about what the neighbors would say. I don't know if he will go for it, but let's see. I'd feel perfectly comfortable staying with you. You're like grandparents I don't have."

"I'm confident they'll do anything to have you closer. Give it a try. Tell them to call me, and we can talk about it with them. Johnny, I think it's a plan."

I hang up, and Mom enters the room first, asking if Dad can come in. I can't believe he continues to ask me. That is different, for sure. I'm glad they are here because we can talk about what to do.

"Mom, Dad, I have an idea about coming home."

I share my conversation with the Olsons. Mom and Dad are both smiling, and no one is getting angry. That's a great sign. I ended by saying that Mr. Olson said they could call him and discuss it further if they would like.

"Well, what do you think? Would it work for me to stay with the Olsons?"

Mom speaks first without even looking at Dad. Impressive that she is making her own decision.

"Yes, yes, yes! Whatever you need. George and Millie have become friends of ours. We trust them. If they want to help, I think we let them. We can make this a transition of sorts and we can start over. Robert, what do you think?"

"Johnny, I'll do anything. Yes. Let me call George and talk with them."

Wow, that was easier than I thought it would be. Dad calls Mr. Olson and they all agree I can go there and live until I decide I'm ready to go home. It's all my decision.

Maybe things really will be different.

Chapter 21

"Maggie, can I admit something to you?"

"You can tell me anything."

"I was disappointed when Johnny presented the plan to go live with George and Millie. I bit my tongue to keep from telling him that he needed to come home and show us some respect."

"Saying that would have driven him even further away."

"I know, but it isn't easy doing nothing. This is all new for me, and I'm afraid I'm going to mess it all up again. Nothing about this is normal. Since when does a son dictate to his parents where he'll live?"

"Fathers don't normally hit their children and their wives. We haven't been a normal family, despite how much you wanted the world to believe it. You're slipping into denial mode again. I'll take part of the blame. This is *our* fault, not his. We're all going to have to learn to think and act differently."

"There's an AA meeting at noon."

#

"My name is Robert, and I'm an alcoholic. My son was in a terrible accident a few days ago, and it's my fault." I share the story with everyone.

The next man in the circle, an older man, speaks up. "I'm Dan; I'm an alcoholic. When I had to put my family back together, I had to remember that the only father my children knew at the time was a drunk one. Like your son, my children were afraid of me, and for good reason. When I got sober, it took my son a year before he'd agree to see me at all. He was almost 20 years old. Learning how to control my impulses and my actions didn't come overnight."

Another member says, "Focus on yourself, and he'll come around. I have to constantly tell myself to stay off the pity pot and make my amends."

Listening to all the stories, I am struck by the honesty of these people. Hearing their stories makes me feel less guilty and helps me realize I am at least a "normal" alcoholic. We go around the circle, and each person takes their turn, some people.

The last young man looks at me and says, "The most important thing I've learned here in the past year is that this program is about more than not taking a drink. To stay sober, we've got to understand why we drank, what we were trying to hide, and why we gave a liquid so much power over us. I drank to hide, to give myself the courage to do what I felt I needed to do. I couldn't control myself, so I used booze to do it. Now, I can't use booze to give me courage and hide behind. I've had to learn how to cope like other people. I must control my temper, be humble, and let go of many things. I have to be honest not only with others but also with myself. It's such a different way to live."

It strikes me that while I haven't had a drink in months, I've only started this journey toward change. After everyone speaks, my sponsor, Andrew, gets up and walks toward me with his hand in his pocket.

"One more thing, Robert. I have something special to give you. This coin represents the 90 days you've been sober. Keep it in your pocket; use it to remind you of the 12 steps and keep you centered. I still carry my first coin, and the writing is nearly worn off after 15 years."

He hands me the coin; I rub it and put it in my pocket. I want to show it to Johnny as proof. Then I realize this is not an honor or something to show off. I slip it into my pocket.

#

The next morning, we go to the hospital to see Johnny and the doctor walks in.

"Johnny, I think you'll be ready to go home the day after tomorrow if you can keep up the physical therapy and continue to improve. You're a strong and healthy young man, and you will be able to do anything you can with that cast. You may have a few headaches, but your doctor at home should be able to watch you. We'll send home all the notes. You'll be able to take the cast off in about four weeks, and hopefully, you won't need any additional physical therapy."

The doctor leaves. While I agreed he could live at the Olsons', I want him to come home. I take a deep breath and remind myself that I need to have patience, and at least he'll be down the street. Johnny is excited about going to the Olsons', and they've proven to be good friends. This is the best plan.

Mike walks in, and Johnny quickly tells him he'll be leaving the hospital and shares the plan to live with the Olsons'.

"Johnny, you need to know that your parents are being understanding with you, and that is worth something."

Johnny looks at me and says, "Dad, you're being understanding; I like the new you."

My heart melted; I needed to hear this.

"George and Millie have the same goals we have. They'll be supportive and helpful to all of us. This is a plan."

#

As I lie down to sleep, I review our plan. We'll drive to the airport, fly to St. Louis, and drive to the Olson's together. I'm going to focus on how wonderful it is that Johnny will be living near us and we can rebuild. I'm thankful to be sober, and I see hope in our future.

#

"Well, son, are you ready to come back to Missouri?"

"Yes, Dad, I am. Can we stop by the ranch to say goodbye?

"I talked to Mike before I came, and they're expecting you. You've got a few things to pick up, right?"

"Not much, but yes. I need to say thank you and goodbye to Flash as well."

We load into the rental car and drive to the stables. I thank Mike and Johnny's friends. They have sincerely helped save our family. I owe them a lot as they cared for, protected, and saved Johnny's life. I catch Mike and take him aside.

"Mike, I have to show you this; no one else understands the value."

I pull out my token.

"It's a start, Robert; be proud, but know it's only a beginning."

"I want to share this with Johnny, but I realize it proves nothing and is a reminder for me. What do you think?"

"Share everything with Johnny. There is no better way to teach him than by letting him share this journey, even the hard stuff. Not only will it help build trust but maybe it can break the cycle of this disease between generations. You and I both know firsthand that he is also in danger."

"Thank you for the advice. I'll share, not as any kind of proof, but as a commitment to being open and honest with him. This may be a small, simple coin, but it means more to me than any of the plagues on my office wall. I have full intention of earning many more, one day at a time."

After Johnny says his goodbye, we drive to Denver to catch a plane. The three of us are together on our way back home. We laugh and listen to Margaret sing. It had been years since I heard her sing; it was music to my ears. Johnny is in the back with his leg propped up across the seat. He quietly drifts to sleep. He has much healing to do, and so do I.

"Maggie, I know this isn't going to be easy, but we have our boy safe and near. I'm going to need your help as I know we will now be facing everyday problems, and I can't use my drinking to help me cope anymore. I also know my law practice has suffered and I'm going to have to give Justin and Sean an explanation."

"What will you tell them, Robert?"

"I'll need to be honest with them. I no longer aspire to be elected for anything; I want to focus on being a good father and husband. I want to watch Johnny grow into a better man than I can ever be. He is strong, smart, and so brave. You have both given me another chance. I have hurt you both in every possible way."

"I believe in you and I'm going to continue to learn how I can be supportive of you. I've supported you in the past by hiding things and getting you drinks. I'll be more courageous and hold up a mirror so you can stay accountable. I'm learning as well."

"I'm falling in love with you all over again."

We arrive at the airport, and with the help of a wheelchair, we can all board the plane back to St Louis. Months of worry and searching have brought us back. We get our car and drive to the Olsons'.

"George has become like a father to me in many ways. He has shown us unconditional support. Johnny, I know you have loved him for a long time. I'm so thankful for all he has given you. Without George's teaching, you may not have survived this journey."

We pull up to the Olson's home, and they have a "welcome home" banner hanging on the porch. They greet Johnny with a hug, which he warmly returns. He'll be safe and happy here. I'm committed to going slowly and letting him lead the way. We discuss plans for the Olsons and Johnny to come over in three days for dinner. Margaret is planning on cooking all of Johnny's favorites.

#

I have invited my law partners, Justin and Sean, as well as all the staff and paralegals in the practice, to a meeting this morning. They surprise me with a banner welcoming me back.

"I want to thank everyone for all your support this summer. Cards, letters, calls, and texts meant the world to us. I know you worked hard to cover my clients and cases, and I'll never be able to repay you. I want to share with you all the details of the summer and ask for your help as my family gets rebuilt."

I proceed to tell the story of the summer, including my alcoholism and my commitment to never drink again. Everyone listens. I'm amazed that no one laughs at me; everyone is very supportive. Afterward, I receive many handshakes and hugs of support.

Justin walks into my office.

"You should know that I'm also a friend of Bill W, and I've been sober for 6 years."

"I had no idea."

"I want you to know that I promise I'll be here for you. Here is a printed copy of the serenity prayer. I've had this framed copy on my desk for the last 6 years. I now share it with you. It kept me calm and even kept me from drinking on more than one occasion. I'm here if you need anything."

I know, at this moment, I need to take down the plaques from my wall. These wooden symbols aren't important; it is Johnny and Maggie that matter. I place a photo we took when we left the hospital on my desk, right next to Justin's framed copy of the serenity prayer.

Chapter 22

Mom and Dad pick me up from the hospital and drive me to the ranch. I have to collect my belongings and say goodbye to Mike and the guys. I found a home and a family here. I love riding and working in the stables. I grab my crutches and manage to get out of the backseat of the car. I hobble over to see Flash before I go. I hand him a carrot.

"Thank you, Flash, for saving my life. You've got a special place in my heart."

Mike walks into the stable and puts his arm around my neck.

"Johnny, you've done a great job this summer, especially for a kid who had never met a horse." We both laugh, and he rubs the top of my head.

"You know you can call me anytime. I'm still with you even if you're not here. You have a job waiting for you here next year if you like and your parents approve. Flash will be here waiting for you. Consider this your summer home. Work hard in school. I want to hear how you're doing. You're so smart. Go to college. Someday, you can take over this stable, heck, even the entire hotel, as smart as you are. This isn't goodbye."

"Mike, I can't thank you and Waldo enough. You believed in me and have guided and protected me. I'll plan on returning next summer but in the meantime, I'll be working hard to accept the things I can't change and change the things I can, just like the serenity prayer you taught me says. I'll keep you up to date on how things are going."

The other guys walk in and hand me a gift. They all take turns hugging me. I open the gift and we all laugh. It is a bucking bronco statue and engraved below it says, "Jimmy Olson, #1 rider."

I thank them all and assure them I'll be back next summer. They assure me they'll take care of Flash.

Next thing I know, we are pulling up at the Olsons' house. I look at the house, and on the front porch is a banner welcoming me. It says, "Welcome Home, Johnny," and has balloons beside it. I immediately notice that instead of two chairs on the porch, there are three. I get out of the car, and the Olsons greet me with a hug. They show me my room. There are pictures everywhere of me riding Flash. There is also a photo of The Loch on the wall.

"Your dad gave us these pictures for your room. We knew you'd love them."

Did Dad do this? He didn't even tell me so he could take credit.

"Dad, thank you for the photos. I didn't know you took any."

"Mike gave them to me, but I took The Loch one when our family was there before."

"I love it. I appreciate the thought."

Mom and Dad prepare to leave. Mom gives me a big hug and tells me she loves me. Dad shakes my hand. I see tears in his eyes.

"I'm so glad you're back and so thankful you are staying here with the Olsons. Please come by the house anytime; it is your home. We look forward to dinner this week with you all."

Mrs. Olson gets me a slice of fresh pie and a glass of milk. I sit at the table with them.

Mr. Olson says, "We've been talking. Now that you are living here, it's not right you call us Mr. and Mrs. How about you call us Grandma and Grandpa instead? We'd be honored to have those titles."

"Really? Oh, Mr. Olson, I mean Grandpa, that is perfect. Grandma, you make the best pie ever. Thank you both."

I head off to bed. I'm glad to be back in Cape, glad to have my real name back, and glad to have grandparents. School starts in just a couple of weeks. I want this all to work out. Dad says we must go one day at a time, so that is what I'll do.

#

I wake to the smell of bacon. Grandma is making breakfast. Wow!

It seems odd calling Mrs. Olson Grandma, but I love it.

"Good morning, Johnny. I hope you slept well. You were very tired."

"It was a long trip and a long day, but I slept very well in my new room."

"We want you to know you are free to have friends here anytime. You just make this your home; we are going to love having everyone here."

"I guess everyone in town knows about my adventure this summer. What should I tell them when they ask why I left? Dad will be mad if I tell them the truth, but I don't want to have to go back to lying all the time."

"Johnny, you tell the truth. Your Dad has admitted his errors and backed out of politics to focus on himself and your family; you have to feel free to be honest; you don't have to lie anymore. Admitting that something was wrong was the first thing your Dad had to do, so there is no need for lies."

"Do you think he's still going to keep from drinking now that I'm back, or was it just show and things will go back to how they were?"

"Johnny, we saw how worried your dad was when you left. We sat with your parents for several days, watching their desperation to find you. I sure hope that losing you was enough of a scare that he will stay the course. Time will tell."

"I sure hope so, but I just can't trust him yet; it's too good to be true."

There is a knock at the door, so I go to see who it is.

"Tommy, Sam, so glad to see you!"

"Johnny, we heard you are back, so we came to find out all about your adventure. You are a star. We saw the paper and the TV news; you were the talk of the town. Someone said you are living here."

"Well, it was quite an adventure, for sure. Come on in. Grandma has just finished baking some muffins; would you like some?"

"Oh yes!"

We walk into the kitchen, and the smell of blueberry muffins permeates the room. We sit down, and Grandma gets everyone muffins and milk.

I'm so proud this is my home; I love having friends to share it with.

"Johnny, tell us about your summer. How did you build that raft anyway?"

"I had gotten instructions from the Internet during study hall last spring. I studied them and worked in a cave on the bluffs until it was finished. I wish I had a photo."

"We can't imagine how in the world you did it! And going down the river and crashing. Were you scared?"

"I'm not going to lie. I was terrified, especially when a snake swam by."

"Johnny, why did you do it; why did you run away? I also get mad at my dad, but I don't think I could ever leave."

"My dad drank too much. He was a drunk and beat my mom and sometimes me. Now he's trying again. I hope he stays in recovery, but not everyone does. Until I can trust him again, I'm staying here with Grandpa and Grandma."

"That's perfect; we can have muffins all the time. These are awesome,

Mrs. Olson, thank you."

"We want to help you, Johnny. We don't want you to run away again. What can we do for you?"

"It's just great to see you guys and have some friends my age. Would you guys like to see my cave? I'm slow but pretty good on these crutches."

"Sure, let's go!"

"Grandma, is it ok if we go to the cave? I promise I'm not up to anything."

She smiles and giggles.

"How about you take Grandpa too? He'd love to see it; then we will know where to come and find you."

#

We walk to the entrance of the cave. I bend over to walk in, and the old, familiar, damp smell brings back many memories. I spot my toolbox is still against the wall, just as I left it.

Grandpa looks over at me and smiles. "Johnny, this is an awesome place. I love how you have used the branches to carpet the floors."

I show them my toolbox and begin describing my building process and plans.

"I'd like for us to use the cave as our secret clubhouse. We can meet here and have a great time, just us, no one else."

"What a perfect plan! Sam and I won't share the location with anyone."

"Just as long as someone knows where you are. Johnny, whenever you come here, please share that with Grandma and me."

I showed everyone the path I had made down the hill and the place I built the raft. I didn't think I would ever be back here, but here I am. The difference this time is I need it for safety, only fun.

I tell them about rafting down the river, including the snakes, the farmer on the side of the river, and the river itself. I talk about hitchhiking and Waldo and the trip to Colorado.

"I was pretty well prepared except for sunscreen. I've thought a lot about whether I would do it all over under the same circumstances, and the answer is yes. Things at home were bad and very tense. I was terrified. I have no regrets; I don't."

Sam asks, "Do you think things have changed? Do you trust your father?"

"Not yet, Sam. Dad's trying, I know, but only time will tell. He gave up the election and he has new friends. He and Mom seem in love again. I know he goes to meetings. I'm going to start going to Al-Anon for family members. I'm going to take it one day at a time. I'm lucky to have Grandma and Grandpa to take care of me and give me a great home until I feel okay to go back."

"Tommy and I are here for you, as well. We don't know a lot about alcohol, but we can be your eyes and ears around town, and we are here for you to talk to."

I'm glad school is starting; I'm hopeful I can have friends now that I can be honest about my life and have a great place to invite guys over.

We walk back home to Grandma and Grandpa's. After the guys leave and we are eating lunch, the kitchen gets quiet.

Grandpa reaches over and takes my hand.

"Johnny, I don't want you to ever be afraid again. We're so sorry that you had to go through all those years of trouble. I'm sorry I didn't notice anything was wrong; I assure you I would have called the authorities if I had known. Both you and your parents were really good actors."

"I agree with Grandpa. I feel just terrible that I didn't notice. We will never let anything like that happen again, we promise."

"It's solely mom and dad's fault, not yours. Mom is also to blame, as she didn't protect me; in fact lied time and time again to cover Dad. Dad says he learned from his father, but I think that's a cop-out. I'll never be like him. How could he have gone through what I have and not changed? The Al-Anon pamphlet says that it's common that alcohol and abuse travel from one generation to another, but I'll never treat anyone the way Dad does. I'll protect my children even from their parents. Mike and the guys taught me compassion and respect. You are both teaching me what it means to love someone and take care of them. Dad has a lot to learn."

"We intend to help your dad learn. He seems to trust us and is willing to listen. I can help you by also helping him, but never think that I'm on his side or not protecting you. Please promise to trust me."

"I do trust you, Grandpa, and now that it's all in the open, I can trust you more. I couldn't before because I dared not tell anyone. Dad would have killed me. If for no other reason, I did the right thing running away because now all the secrecy is gone, the world knows him for who he is."

#

Two weeks later, the phone rings; it's Mike and the guys.

"Hi, Jimmy, or I mean Johnny! How are you? We miss that smile; Flash told us to give you a call and check-in."

"So good to hear you guys. Things are awesome here. The Olsons told me to call them Grandma and Grandpa. My room is perfect, I love school, and I have new friends."

"That's great. Have you gone to Al-Anon yet, like I suggested?"

"I'm going tonight. Mom is coming with me. I'm nervous. I talked to the counselor about it today at school. I'm sure it will become easier. I'm looking forward to meeting some other guys who have similar fathers."

"I'm glad you are going, Johnny. I wish my family had agreed to go years back. My brother Waldo was the only one. He says to tell you hello and to insist you call him. He said he's not out of your life just because I stepped in."

We laugh at Waldo.

"Mike, I still plan on coming out this summer and working, so save me a spot. Give Flash a carrot for me."

"You have a spot no worry, we will take care of the details this spring. In the meantime, you stay in touch with us; I'll send you some photos of Flash."

"I'd love that. He saved my life; he gives me hope."

"Bye, for now, Johnny, take care of yourself. We are here if you need us. Enjoy Alanon."

#

Mom picks me up at Grandma and Grandpa's, and we drive in near silence to the meeting. The AA group is meeting in the same church building downstairs, but Mom has promised Dad will not approach me there; he is giving me space.

We get out of the car; my hands are sweating, and my legs are weak. Part of me wants to hide in the car. The old me would have done just that. In contrast, the stronger me yearns for others to share with, to find out if my story is unique or if other fathers are like mine and what people do about it. I take a deep breath as I walk in. There are people of all ages there. I glance over, and I see a girl from school there with her mom.

That's Angela; is her Dad a drunk too? Wow.

I leave Mom and go over to see Angela.

"Hi, Angela. I'm surprised to see you here. I didn't know."

"Hi, Johnny. I heard about your summer and was hoping someone would lead you here. It's not like we can talk about this very easily at school. I'm glad you came."

"Have you been coming here long?"

"I started coming here with Mom two years ago. My Dad was still drinking when we first came. The group helped us learn how to deal with him, how to protect ourselves, and how to draw boundaries. It's the reason I didn't run away myself."

"Wow, that's encouraging."

"Where is the AA meeting? I don't want to see my dad tonight."

"No fear; there is a separate entrance, and they are all told not to come upstairs. That part gets easier, but I sure understand your concerns."

I grab a bottle of water, and Mom comes to sit by me.

If I were smaller, I'd take her hand. I'm so nervous.

The leader reads out of a book. Angela's mom talks first, which means I talk last.

"Hi, I'm Grace, and I'm here with my daughter Angela. I'm the wife of an alcoholic."

"Hi, Grace."

"I started coming here two years ago while my husband was still drinking. I'm glad to say he's getting his 12-month coin tonight. It took a year once I learned not to take care of him, make excuses for him, and put myself and Angela first. Once he had to pay the consequences for his actions, he hit bottom and agreed to come. But it was not easy, and if I'm honest, I still watch him every day for signs he's drinking again. I've learned to forgive myself for letting him do what he did to Angela and me. I know better now that it will never happen again. I can't control him, but I can control my reaction to him. He had to quit for him. I didn't threaten; I just stood tall. No more calls telling his boss he was sick, no more excuses with friends. I quit hiding the truth. I'm thankful for this group and all I have learned."

Similar stories as everyone went around the circle. One teenage guy across the table said he had run away. He was only gone one night before the cops found him and brought him home. I'd like to hear more about that story.

"Hello, my name is Margaret, and my husband, Robert, is an alcoholic. This is my first time here, but I can relate to almost every story. My husband has only been sober for a couple of months. It's like I'm meeting him for the first time. I still find myself worried he'll be upset with me. I search for alcohol in all his old hiding places, expecting to find it. So far, so good; can this be it?"

"Hello, I'm Johnny, and my dad is an alcoholic. Things were so bad I ran away last summer. I'm not living at home yet because I don't trust either mom or dad. I'm safe and happy with Grandma and Grandpa, and I don't know when I might go back or if I will ever go back to that house, which was never a home."

On the drive back home, Mom is pretty quiet.

"Mom, what did you think of the meeting?"

"There are a lot of people in the same place we are. I'm just so sorry I didn't come before. I'm so sorry I was not brave enough to protect you. I thought I was protecting you by letting him hurt me instead any time I could. I now understand that was not helping either of us. Johnny, I want to be a better mom; I want you to trust that I will keep you safe. I want to grow as Angela's mom has. I promise I'm going to try. Grace and I exchanged phone numbers and are going to go to lunch once a week."

"Mom, I'm so glad. This will be good for both of us, regardless of what Dad chooses to do. I learned tonight that he has to take care of him. We have to live our lives and not let him determine our happiness. I loved it, and I look forward to becoming friends with Angela and meeting that other guy across the table who ran away. I wish I had known them before. I also must admit I'm pretty proud I was more successful at escaping."

#

School is going well. I see the counselor once a week. I've gotten into reading; the librarian knows I like stories about animals, especially horses, and she gives me great suggestions. I'm making good grades and love my classes.

Every week, Grandma, Grandpa, and I go to Mom and Dad's for dinner at least once. Tonight, Grandma and Grandpa drive me to the house, and it has Christmas lights all over it. There is Christmas music playing outside and a wreath on the door. I run into the house and hug Mom.

"I love it. We've never had decorations." I run through the house and notice the tree by the fireplace. On the chimney mantel, I notice three Christmas stockings with our names on them. They all match. My house has never looked like this. It's not a museum anymore.

We sit down to dinner and Dad says grace (also something new).

"Robert and I were hoping you would all come for Christmas here. Johnny, we were hoping you might spend the night in your old room on Christmas Eve. George and Mary, we'd love it if you stayed in the guest room right next to Johnny's room. This way, we could all have

Christmas morning together."

I didn't expect that; what would it be like to stay here again?

Dad says, "Johnny, why don't you and I paint your room this weekend? You can pick out the color."

Mom adds, "Why don't you and I go shopping for some new things for your room? You can decide what kind of a theme you want, and we will fix it all up."

I remember someone talking about a similar thing at Al-Anon. "I'd like to think about all that, as they are big steps. I do like the idea of a new room and leaving the old one behind. I'm not sure how I feel about spending the night or painting with your Dad. Let's talk more about it next week at dinner."

Breathe; I stood my ground, and no one acted upset or disappointed. Good job.

Tonight, as I lay in bed, I think about how different things are this Christmas than last year. Dad has stayed involved in AA and has fun friends. I have made friends with the kids of some of his AA friends at various social activities. Mom is happy; she sings and laughs. The house is decorated for Christmas for the first time. I get to make choices for a new room. When I made my escape, the house was like a museum. I felt no joy and no love inside. Now, I smile when I walk in, and love is everywhere.

#

Because I trust Grandma and Grandpa, I decided to do the Christmas Eve overnight. There is no drama, only family time. I'm not afraid. There is hope, after all.

Chapter 23

"Johnny, I'd like it if you would come to my AA meeting with me today. It's a special day as I celebrate my 1 year of sobriety. Friends and family can attend these meetings, as they are open meetings. Would you honor me by attending as I share my story?"

"Dad, you want me to go after everything that happened after I ran away a year ago?"

"Son, you are the one that jolted me into admitting I had a problem. You are the one who was brave enough to draw a line and make me face the reality of what I was doing to myself and our family. This is not a celebration because my fight with this disease will last a lifetime. It is a recognition that I have managed the first year and a way to remember the story so I never go back to that dark place."

"Dad, I would love to come."

We arrive at the meeting, and I introduce Johnny to my new friends.

They are quite different from the ones I had before I stopped drinking. There are no suits here. There are no pretenders. They are young and old, wealthy and poor. This disease crosses all aspects of life. I find myself shaking as they call my name and ask me to speak tonight. The hall is quiet as I rise and go to the front of the room.,

"My name is Robert; I'm a grateful alcoholic."

"Hi, Robert."

"I look across this room and see many new friends; for this, I am thankful. I never believed that people could like me for all that I am. I no longer have secrets; all my character defects are exposed and open. I appreciate your acceptance and guidance as I continue to face this baffling, cunning disease every day."

I look around and take a deep breath.

"Today is my 12-month anniversary. I didn't think I'd ever go 12 hours without a drink, let alone 12 months. I also didn't think life would be any fun without alcohol. Since I put that bottle down, my life has changed. I feel like a young man again. I see my wife in a different light. It's like we are dating again. My son looks at me with new eyes. I love my job and people have embraced my character defects since I admit to them rather than try to hide them. One year ago, my son ran away, I thought he was dead, and I'd never see him again. I was so concerned about the opinion of others that I lost myself and buried my fears in booze. I'm glad to be alive."

I see Johnny looking at the ground in deep reflection. *What is he thinking? Is he embarrassed about my past?*

My sponsor walks up and hands me the precious 12-month coin. Such a simple object, but it symbolizes everything to me. I've never worked harder for anything. I put it in my pocket and rub it gently. Someday, I'll have one with XV on it, like my sponsor, Dave. One day at a time.

Johnny and I walk home from the meeting.

"Dad, did you mean it? Do you and Mom feel like you are dating again? I see you smile at her and tease her, and it makes me happy. I notice you don't fight, but I thought perhaps you just didn't want me to know."

"Johnny, I love your mother more today than ever in our life. She has stood by me, and she makes me a better man. I was awful to her, and I know it. It hurts my heart to think of those times. But AA helped me to make amends to her, to ask her forgiveness, and to promise to be a better husband. I am a lucky man, most of those people at the meeting lost their family, but I have a second chance."

"Dad, this is one of the best days in my life. I never believed I could hear you talk like that."

Johnny goes back to the Olsons' for the night. Margaret and I sit down after dinner with a glass of iced tea.

"Tomorrow morning, we are taking Johnny to Colorado to spend the summer with Mike and the guys; are you worried about it, Maggie?"

"I'm not. I know he's in good hands; they will watch over him as they did last year."

"I know I promised him he could do this; I just remember the pain of a year ago. The fear of him being dead on the river."

"If we want him to trust us, we must trust him, Robert. He's 15 now and halfway through high school. He's shown us he can make it, and we must let him continue to grow."

Suddenly, I'm overwhelmed. I want a drink so bad I can taste it. I reach into my pocket and rub the new coin.

Johnny is leaving; what if he doesn't return? What if he has another accident like last year? What if he loves Mike more than me? Mike is certainly a good man.

Margaret goes on to bed, and I peek in on her and find her asleep. I creep up the stairs to the attic. I open the door quietly so Maggie doesn't hear me. I go to the trunk and slowly lift the bottle out.

Just one drink doesn't have to be a big one. One drink won't hurt anything. No one will even know.

I realize I forgot a glass. If I go back downstairs, I might get caught, so I'll take a quick swig from the bottle. I unscrew the lid and smell. Wow, it smells like heaven. I forgot how I love that smell. It's been 12 months. Only once have I even touched a bottle, and that was early, and I resisted. Here it is in my hands, top off, ready to put up to my mouth. I'll tip my head back, take one swig, and put the bottle back. No one will be the wiser.

Why do you want to ruin everything now? What good would one drink do anyway? No one else would know, but I would.

Quickly, I screw the lid back on and put the bottle back in the trunk and shut the lid. I take a big breath. Slowly and quietly, I walk down the steps. I go outside and call Dave—confession time.

I go for a walk and am relieved that I did not fall off the wagon. My sponsor, Dave helped me to process what happened. Dave is supportive and yet gives me a warning.

"Robert, sobriety is a lifelong journey; just because it's been a year and we acknowledge it does not mean you are not vulnerable; in fact, you may be more vulnerable as time goes along. Be careful to remain humble and remember you are powerless against alcohol. Rest assured, you are not the only one to be tempted on an anniversary. Turn to your higher power, feed off that strength, and redirect your thoughts from 'stinkin' thinkin'.'"

"Thanks, Dave; this journey has only just begun, but I'm committed."

George and Mary Olson, Maggie, and I drive Johnny to Colorado. We laugh and tell stories. We pull into the ranch about dinner time. Mike has the grill going and we can smell the ribs before we can see anyone. Johnny jumps out of the car and hugs Mike and the guys. He runs over and sees Flash having some important conversation with the horse, giving him a carrot and returning. What teenager wouldn't enjoy this place for the summer? Johnny is in good hands.

Chapter 24

"Mike, I've only been here a week, and it feels like I never left. I'm so excited to be back with everyone."

"We missed you, Johnny. Have you thought about your plans after the summer? Any thoughts about college?"

"Yes, I think I'm ready to move back home this fall. Dad has made it over a year; he and mom seem to be doing well, and I'm better equipped to handle him now that I'm older and have the support of Alanon."

"That is real growth, Johnny. I'm proud of you and your family. Stories don't always turn out this way. How about friends? Do you have any?"

"I have two good friends in Al-Anon, several at school, and two in my neighborhood. It's a big difference from last year. One of my Al-

Anon friends is my girlfriend. Her father is an alcoholic also. She has been going to Al-Anon for a long time. Her Dad even had a slip and started drinking again, but she and her mom had help handling it, and her dad is sober once again. That also gives me hope."

"As I told your father, sobriety is a lifelong journey, and he has only started. Your family is doing a great job building up the tools needed to continue the journey. What about college? Have you thought about it?"

"I want to go to the University of Missouri. They not only have a veterinary medicine program but also an Equine teaching facility in which I can participate as an undergraduate. I was told it's more difficult to get admitted to vet school than medical school. I figure all my summers here will give me excellent experience and help me get admitted. I'm going to need outstanding grades, but I know I can do it."

"Johnny, that is wonderful. I'll help in any way I can. You should be sure and work some with our vet each summer; I'll introduce you."

I walk over and sit on the fence, and Flash stops in front of me. I hand him the daily carrot I give him.

"Flash, I think of you every day. You saved my life, and I'll never forget."

#

I rode Flash every day this summer. I took care of his stall and told him all my dreams and fears. Funny how I can tell Flash things I can't say to anyone else. I love the way he tilts his head as I hand him a carrot. The summer is ending, and I must go back to school. I look forward to coming back next summer.

On the way back to Missouri, Mom, Dad, and I talk.

"Johnny, we are so glad you had such a great summer here, we know you are excited to come back again next year. This is such a great experience for you, the perfect summer job."

"I've decided to go to MU for college. I want to be a veterinarian, and Mike said he would help write me a letter. My summers with him will be so helpful in getting admitted. Mike told me vet school is harder to get into than medical school, but I'm determined."

"Johnny, we will do everything we can to support you. I think that's an excellent choice."

"Dad, is it okay if I move back home this year? I've been thinking, and I'm ready for us to be a real family again. Grandma and Grandpa will still be close and they said I can spend as much time there as I want to. I thought next weekend we could move my stuff."

"Of course, that is the best news ever!"

#

It's late on October 30, the night before Halloween. I finish my homework and am getting ready for bed. I heard Dad answer the phone and say he'd come get me. He walks into my room with an alarmed and sad look on his face.

"Mike is on the phone; it's important you speak with him."

"Johnny, we found Flash lying in his stall tonight when we went to feed him. I'm sorry to tell you he has died. He had been acting a bit odd, but we didn't think anything of it. The vet said he went suddenly and did not suffer. I wanted you to be the first to know. Flash loved you, don't ever doubt that."

"Mike, this can't be. He can't be gone."

Tears begin falling. I am in disbelief. Flash meant everything to me; he saved my life and taught me to trust again.

I hang up the phone, and Dad comes up to me and puts his arms around me. I sob in the comfort of his arms. I can't quit crying.

"Johnny, I understand. Flash was like a part of the family. I know you loved him. Tell me about him; tell me again the story of when you were first learning to ride."

Dad and Mom listen to my stories and my love for Flash for hours. I feel better having shared it. They suggest we have a little memorial for him in a couple of days with Grandma and Grandpa and even Mike and the boys via Zoom.

#

I gather all my photos of me and Flash and set them on the dining room table. Mom, Dad, Grandma, and Grandpa sit around me, and Mike and the boys are on the computer on the table so they can feel like they are a part of everything. Dad points the camera at me so I can say the few words I prepared.

"Flash was a great horse; he was loyal and very patient with me. He knew all my secrets and loved me anyway, or maybe it was the carrots I gave him. I'm glad he did not suffer and died suddenly, although I sure wish I could have had one last pet and said goodbye. Wherever you are Flash, I want you to know that you will remain a part of my life, my memory. I am going to graduate as a veterinarian and help other horses in your honor. You are the reason."

Others share fond memories, and we have a moment of silence.

It won't be the same on the ranch without him.

[Insert image-Ranch?]

Chapter 25

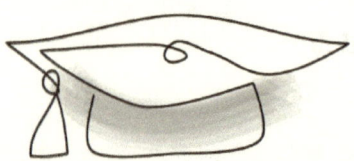

It's a beautiful sunny day with a light breeze in May. I had my 24th birthday yesterday. The vet school graduation is May 12th on the quad at the University of Missouri. I stand beside the stage in a black robe, adjusting the square board on my head and its dangling yellow tassel, waiting for my name to be called. I pause, and then I hear it.

"Doctor John Westwood."

I walk up the stairs, take the piece of parchment, and shake the extended hand. I walk down the opposite stairway. It's done; school is now done; I'm Dr. Westwood.

I pause for the official graduation photo and look to the sky. I raise my diploma and smile at Flash. I know he's watching.

I remove the robe and walk across the street to The Heidelberg, my favorite Columbia hang-out. Dad reserved the rooftop for our private celebration. After I walk up the stairs, I see him standing proudly, arms extended. He embraces me, tears in his eyes.

"John, we are so proud of you!"

"Thank you, Dad, and thanks for this party."

Everyone takes a seat, and the celebration begins. Several individuals rise and make toasts of congratulations, most with non-alcoholic beer. After all the fanfare, I rise and hold my glass high in the air.

"There aren't enough words to thank everyone here today for getting me to this point. Thanks to Mom and Dad for this party." I lean over and give them both a hug.

"In this same month of May, twelve years ago, I was rafting down the Mississippi River. A young, determined, scared-to-death teenager, I never dreamed I would be standing in this place, surrounded with so much love, and looking at such a perfect future. Dad, I admire your courage to change and your strength to turn your life around.

"Mom, I have watched you every day laugh and sing, and it brings me joy. Grace, you are a gift to my mom, her best friend and her life coach, showing her how to be supportive of Dad, but not responsible for him." Everyone laughs.

"There are no words for Grandma and Grandpa and their selfless support of me for as long as I can remember. Standing in the garage learning how to tie knots, watching their warmth and affection toward one another, and above all else, finding a place in their home when I needed it most completely changed the life of our family.

"Waldo, to this day, I can't believe how lucky I was that it was you who picked me up off the highway. You were wise, understanding, and helpful. You allowed me to trust again. You were on the other end of the phone, orchestrating my safety the entire summer.

Mike, you opened your heart to this scared, confused kid and showed me the hope that recovery would save my family. I'm also lucky you are here to celebrate with us. I look forward to our new partnership with the ranch and clinic in Estes Park. No other graduate today will be starting off as lucky as I am. The Flash Equine Clinic will be our legacy together. I'm so lucky. Because of you, my son will grow to know the glory of riding and the wonder of the mountains.

"Lastly, thank you to my beautiful wife, Angela. Angela, you are positively glowing as you carry our son. I fell in love with you the moment I saw you at the Al-Anon meeting. You were the first person my age with an alcoholic family, and you showed me I was not alone.

After that day, I never felt alone again, all thanks to your friendship. We shared our secrets, we faced our own imperfections, and we created a new path for our generation. Thank you for loving me, for standing by me, and for sharing my life.

"Now, let's eat!"

www.ingramcontent.com/pod-product-compliance
Lightning Source LLC
Chambersburg PA
CBHW031505120626
46545CB00005B/1766